Meet the Mustang Sallies . . .

* Hillary Clinton, U.S. Senator

* Erin Brockovich, activist

* Janet Reno,
  former U.S. Attorney General

* Susan Sarandon,
  Academy Award–winning actress

* Interior Secretary Gale Norton

* Ann Richards,
  former Texas Governor

* Christine Todd Whitman,
  former N.J. governor
  and EPA chief

* Mary Higgins Clark, author

* Cokie Roberts,
  broadcaster and author

* Meg Whitman, CEO of ebay

* Christiane Northrup,
  author and physician

* Pat Mitchell,
  president and CEO of PBS

* Geraldine Laybourne,
  CEO of Oxygen network

* Arianna Huffington,
  author, columnist, and activist

* Gail Collins, editorial page editor
  of *The New York Times*

* Bernadine Healy,
  former chief of the
  American Red Cross

* Gen. Claudia Kennedy,
  the U.S. Army's first woman
  three-star general

* Eve Ensler,
  the author of the acclaimed
  Vagina Monologues

* Secretary of Labor Elaine Chao

* Coleen Rowley,
  the "FBI whistleblower"

* Pat Heim, author and consultant

* Martina Navratilova,
  tennis legend

* Betsy Bernard, president of AT&T

* Sherron Watkins,
  the Enron whistleblower

* Carly Fiorina,
  CEO of Hewlett-Packard

* Sandra Bernhard,
  comedian and actress

* Brett Butler, actress and comedian

* Jane Smith, president,
  Business and Professional Women
  USA

* Kathleen Carroll, executive editor
  of the Associated Press

* Kim Campbell,
  former prime minister of Canada

* Joan Armatrading, singer

* Lenora Cole, former head of the U.S. Department of Labor's woman's bureau,

* Pam Iorio, mayor of Tampa

* Sam Horn, author

* Tracie Cone, publisher

* Laura Ingraham, talk radio host

* Janet Robinson, president of The New York Times Co.

* Carnie Wilson, singer

* Alexa Canady, the first woman and African American neurosurgeon

* Marva Collins, famed educator

* Nadia Comaneci, the Olympic legend

* Nancy Hopkins, the MIT trailblazing professor

* Consuelo Kickbush, Lieutenant Colonel, U.S. Army (ret.)

* Marianne LaFrance, psychology professor at Yale

* Mavis Leno, actist

* Yolanda Moses, president of the American Association of Higher Education

* Sally Priesand, first woman ordained as a rabbi

* Alice Rivlin, former vice-chair of the Federal Reserve

* Esmeralda Santiago, author

* Alex Sink, banking trailblazer

* Elizabeth Roberts, editor

* Ann Rubenstein Tisch, founder of the Young Women's Leadership School in Harlem

* Gen. Wilma Vaught, president of the Women In Military Service For America Memorial Foundation

* Marie Wilson, president of The White House Project

* Carol Higgins Clark, author

* Sylvia Earle, famed oceanographer

* Nancy Grace, anchorwoman and prosecutor

* Janet Guthrie, first woman to race at the Indianapolis 500

MUSTANG SALLIES

*Success Secrets of Women
Who Refuse to Run
with the Herd*

FAWN GERMER

A Perigee Book

Most Perigee Books are available at special quantity discounts for bulk purchases for sales promotions, premiums, fund-raising or educational use. Special books, or book excerpts, can also be created to fit specific needs.

For details, write: Special Markets, The Berkley Publishing Group, 375 Hudson Street, New York, New York 10014.

A Perigee Book
THE BERKLEY PUBLISHING GROUP
Published by the Penguin Group
Penguin Group (USA) Inc.,
375 Hudson Street, New York, New York 10014, USA
Penguin Group (Canada), 10 Alcorn Avenue, Toronto,
Ontario M4V 3B2, Canada (a division of Pearson Penguin Canada Inc.)
Penguin Books Ltd., 80 Strand, London WC2R 0RL, England
Penguin Ireland, 25 St. Stephen's Green, Dublin 2, Ireland (a division of Penguin Books Ltd.)
Penguin Group (Australia), 250 Camberwell Road, Camberwell, Victoria 3124,
Australia (a division of Pearson Australia Group Pty. Ltd.)
Penguin Books India Pvt. Ltd., 11 Community Centre, Panchsheel Park, New Delhi - 110 017, India
Penguin Group (NZ), Cnr Airborne and Rosedale Roads, Albany,
Auckland 1310, New Zealand (a division of Pearson New Zealand Ltd.)
Penguin Books (South Africa) (Pty.) Ltd., 24 Sturdee Avenue, Rosebank, Johannesburg 2196, South Africa

Penguin Books Ltd., Registered Offices:80 Strand, London WC2R 0RL, England

This book is an original publication of The Berkley Publishing Group.

Copyright © 2004 by Fawn Germer
Cover design by Liz Shehan
Cover illustration by Lynn Brown
Text design by Kristin del Rosario

Perigee trade paperback edition: October 2004

Library of Congress Cataloging-in-Publication Data

Germer, Fawn.
   Mustang Sallies / Fawn Germer.—1st Perigee ed.
   p. cm
   "A Perigee book"—T.p. verso.
   ISBN 0-399-53021-5
   1. Women—United States—Psychology. 2. Women—United States—Life skills guides. 3. Women—United States—
Conduct of life. 4. Success—United States. 5. Successful people—United States—Case studies. 6. Self-esteem in
women—United States. I. Title.

HQ1221.G433 2004
6465.7'0082—dc22   2004048353

PRINTED IN THE UNITED STATES OF AMERICA

10 9 8 7 6 5 4 3 2 1

Acknowledgments

IT wasn't that long ago that I was afraid to order an iced tea with dinner because it would add another $2 to the bill. I wasn't a starving author, but close to it. I'd quit my job to chase a dream and, along the way, encountered obstacles so daunting I almost quit.

My friends and family wouldn't let me.

When my first book came out, things started moving very quickly. I was invited to attend the Glamour Woman of the Year Awards in New York, and that was the source of some anxiety because anybody who knows me knows I have no fashion sense and can be quite a klutz if left unsupervised in public. My friends took me shopping and made sure I was ready to mingle with the beautiful people, then sent me off to the big city. The reception around the Temple of Dendur at the Metropolitan Museum of Art was exquisite. I mingled by myself, thinking, *There's Katie Couric! Am I* really *making small talk with Deborah Messing? And there's Diane Sawyer. Wow, her upper arms sure are buff!* It was the most glamorous moment of my life, and there I was, alone, wishing my friends were with me, or that I was with them. It wouldn't matter where.

I am so thankful to have been raised by the greatest mustang alive: my mother, Betty Germer. She told me I could do anything and deserved everything, and sent me out to shake up the world. My father, Fred Germer, is always, *always* there to encourage me to run harder and faster, and taught me to enjoy the challenge for the fun of it all. And my big brother, Jim Germer, has grown into a man I respect and love.

There's my agent, Caroline Carney, a partner and friend who deserves the same unfaltering support she gave me as she chases her own new dream.

At Penguin: My editor, Michelle Howry, is a living model of a mustang with talent, diplomacy, and finesse. Christel Winkler has endured about five years of prank calls from me and *still* helps me out every time I need her. My publisher, John Duff, has made me feel like a member of the family with full voting privileges. The dream team in marketing—Liz Perl, Craig Burke, and Tina Anderson—have promoted my dream as if it were theirs.

There's Jennifer Repo, my former editor who left Penguin but made good on her promise to keep nagging me to stretch.

And, my friends!

Rebecca Whitley, my best friend, who constantly makes me laugh and appreciate all that is good in life. Pam Sarich, who is *there*. Keri Douglas, the most unselfish person I have ever met. Jill Gould, who gave—and gives—me the courage to dare. Trish Goldsmith, Wonder Woman. Tina Proctor, my sidekick. Linda Ambraz and Betsy Pinkerton, who make every trip to Target an adventure. Linda Lindsay, my long lost sister.

My kitchen cabinet: Jonathan Alpert, Connie Bouchard, Carole Cole, Kathy Gaye, Teresa Hoover, Barbara Ropes Pankau, Lisa Rary, and Liz Roberts.

Sam Horn, whose brilliance is only overshadowed by her generosity and warmth.

Mike Hendren, a beautiful man who has taught me so much about faith, love, and friendship.

A few good (and fabulous) men: Chris Broderick, Brian Campbell, George Edmonson, Mike Finney, Joe Moran, Tony Montoya, John Sanko, George Thomas, and David Whitley.

Friends: Christine Bichovsky, Jane Boles, Linda Brown, Susan Edwards, Carol Folsom, Malea Guiriba, Mary Hadar, Martha Kaley, Melissa Katsimpalis, Claudia Kennedy, Betty Klapp, Dana Kuehn, Renee Hardman, Chante Ishta, Carolyn Little, Rachel Moore, Lynn Cotner Rau, Miriam Reed, Linda Robertson, Dorothy Rupert, Laura Sandell,

Alex Sarich, Keri Smith, Judie Taggart, Patricia Tucker, Meredith Tupper, Jackie Walker, and Helen and Jack Whitley.

The Scoobies: Jayne Bray, Betsy Buffo, Lisa Pritchard, and Ron Rowe.

The wild mustangs who have taught me to be bold and brave: Kathy Bowers, Jeanne Elliott, Miriam Reed, and Jackie St. Joan.

New friends: Stan Arthur, Sue Banks, Eric Brown, Mike Cerovac, Leslie Henderson, Brenda Interlandi, Patty Ivey, Pat Jones-Petrick, Charlotte Keane, Eva Krzewinski, Brian Merrill, Kathleen Passanisi, Pam Vaccaro, and Dianne Williams.

My relatives: the Himelhoch, Hirsch, and Rubinstein families.

My troops (who also helped me proofread the book): Linda Ambraz, Vickie Chachere, Susan Edwards, Chris Elsner, Kathy Gaye, Fred Germer, Betty Germer, Trish Goldsmith, Stanley Gray, Susan Gray, Brenda Interlandi, Diane Jamai, Pat Jones-Petrick, Leslie Mizerak, Sue Morrill, Betsy Pinkerton, Lisa Pritchard, Pam Sarich, Judy Wade, Rebecca Whitley, and Jennifer Wise.

And, the most supportive group of neighbors anywhere, many of whom trekked for miles to cheer me on at book signings. Love to the Allen, Ambraz, Baldridge, Elsner, Freshour, Krzeminski, Lee, Linde, Noriega, Pinkerton, Price, Rauh, and Sarich households.

You might not know the people in these acknowledgments, but I wish you did. They make me rich.

*For my loving father, a strong, gentle man
who has proven a million times over
that I am the luckiest daughter in the world.*

Contents

INTRODUCTION

SEVERAL years ago, one of my bosses sat me down in his office and told me, "You've gone as far as you're going to go. All you are now is all you are ever going to be—a reporter." I think of him as "The Tormentor,"—the very opposite of a mentor.

He hated my hard-charging ways and the issues I wanted to cover. I was a mustang, and I didn't know the rules of engagement. I could have avoided a lot of grief had I been coached by the women in this book.

I'll never forget the day when he called me into his office, told me I would no longer cover women's issues, swore my lifelong dream of having a column would "never happen," and told me I wasn't going anywhere. Despite the investigative reporting that had gotten me numerous state and national awards and four Pulitzer nominations, he told me I was to spend more than six weeks writing daily Christmas features, and after that, I'd cover the beat of his choosing. Obviously enjoying his power trip, he would not even deign to tell me what that beat would be. Apparently, since he couldn't tame me, he'd just try to break my spirit.

I felt demoralized, and my self-esteem plunged. My work performance suffered as I slacked off in protest. Finally realizing *I* was turning myself into a victim, I started working hard again. After two years, the metro editor promoted me into management.

I couldn't believe I'd gotten beyond my difficulties until I attended my initial afternoon news meeting with a dozen other editors, including The Tormentor. In that two years, he had moved *way* up the ladder and was now everyone's boss. "Fawn is here today because she's our new night assistant city editor," my metro editor announced. Right in front of everybody, The Tormentor declared, "There's no promotion. She's just a reporter." I just stared, speechless, as I realized there would be no title and no raise—despite what was promised.

After the meeting, I went to my desk, picked up the telephone, and called the editor at another newspaper who had been trying to recruit me for several years. "If you want me," I told him, "make it happen now." He did. I refused to play victim and fired my tormentor.

It took me two days to write the previous six paragraphs. Even though we move on and up, some old lessons are especially hard to learn, and the hurt feelings and anger don't go away just because we ultimately triumph. I was a hard-charging mustang and because of that, I paid a painful price. What I wouldn't have given for the coaching of Ann Richards, Claudia Kennedy, Erin Brockovich, Pat Heim, and the other mustangs I've talked to for the past year. I hope you won't have to pay like I did, which is why I wrote this book. I just want you to know that you are not crazy and you are not alone.

Almost all of the bold, successful women I've interviewed for this book have had soul-challenging experiences like the rest of us and have learned to win in arenas where they were not appreciated or acknowledged. They found ways to overcome their fears and insecurities, and crossed the bridge from being reviled to being revered. They'll tell you that authenticity is not only a challenge, but a reward. You may have been born a mustang, or perhaps the mustang spirit is just starting to stir. Let it live. Every woman can be a mustang. Mustangs aren't just high-profile women in high places. We are everywhere, in every possible socioeconomic class, education level, and rank on the ladder. You may be in organized labor or in the corporate world, in politics or in the arts. I don't care if you work in a law firm or a grocery store, a Fortune 500 company or a Burger King. The mustang spirit lives. Any woman can be a mustang, as long as she dares to be real.

Life is so sweet when you take your power and use it for yourself. If you feel stuck, unstick yourself. Don't listen to your tormentors, and don't torment yourself. You have the right to feel good about who you are, love what you do, and do it well. When you think you are trapped in a bad relationship, you aren't. When you feel sure no one else will want you, they will. If the job is dragging you way down, move on. If you are scared you can't get a job elsewhere, you can. Would I have ever left that job if "The Tormentor" hadn't been so cruel? I'd have missed out on the greatest adventure of my life: writing this. It's amazing. Every time you find yourself in a moment of self-definition, no matter how dark it is, you have the power to turn it into light. Be bold.

1.

ARE YOU A MUSTANG?

"LOWER your voice. Talk slower. Don't be confrontational. Act like you don't know things. Listen. Be awed by the comments made by the other person. . . ."

I am dining in an exquisite restaurant, being mentored by a highly accomplished woman in her 60s. She is telling me how she's accomplished so much in her life without getting labeled "the bitch." "Play the other person up. Make him feel like he is important. Be seated in a way that presents yourself in a more demure manner. Don't be too quick to respond to questions. Use phrases like, 'That's something for me to think about,' or, 'That's a wonderful idea, and I never thought about it,' even if you were the one who invented it in the first place."

I don't know what to say. I can't do any of those things. Not one.

The one thing I absolutely cannot do is mute who I am. I'm a mustang. Mustang Sally, like in the song. Mustangs were the original wild horses of the West. They're tough, strong, agile, sound, and quick to learn. Like the horse, the mustang woman experiences great rewards because her life is filled with surprise, drama, and adventure. She's got guts, because she doesn't run with the herd just because it is easier or more convenient. Convenience is unfulfilling and can be boring. Mustang living is exciting, but can be hard. It can get mighty lonely out there on the trail because there are so many barriers and obstacles to overcome. It can hurt, being viewed as the one on the fringe, especially when some people are so willing to sacrifice heart and soul trying to blend in. Sometimes, our greatest obstacle is the self-doubt that can come when faced with pressure to back down or conform. But it's the trailblazing mustangs who dare to be first, stand up, attack a problem, try a new approach, and keep charging forward despite the inertia or backward movement of the pack.

Sometimes, when it seems like the whole world wants me to slow my mustang down, all I want to do is hit the gas. I've come to realize that chocolate scares the heck out of a world that loves vanilla. I don't know why, but it does. If everyone else is wearing plaid, they are going to hate your polka dots. Some polka-dot lovers will switch to plaid just to fit in, but I'd rather not. I'd much rather be me, perfectly imperfect. I'm the most valuable asset I've got, and if I am going to succeed, I've got to bank on who I really am and charge ahead, flaws and all.

The Mustang Mentality

I spent half of my career trying to figure out what I was doing wrong. Was there some sort of playbook that I didn't get the day I was filling out forms in human resources? Some sort of behavioral code that would have told me how to blend in? I can see the codebook now: "A-team employees are sure to abide, acquiesce, accommodate, and agree. Be a team player by believing, blending, bending, bowing, and buying in. See how you might comply, confer, conform, and concur." No, I never did get my obedience training. What I got was some natural instinct for going boldly where a lot of people wouldn't go, for shaking things up and wondering why the status quo wasn't more appreciative of all my good ideas and honest efforts. I spent a lot of years wallowing in low self-esteem and feeling like an outsider. A misfit.

But, I wasn't a misfit. I was a mustang!

I once told Helen Thomas, the legendary White House journalist, that I have always had trouble shedding the troublemaker label. "I keep being told that I don't know my place," I confided.

"What is your place?" Thomas shot back. "It's what you say it is. It's not what they say it is." Thomas had been through enough battles to know she was and always will be a mustang woman. Until I met her, I didn't realize that's what I was. I'd just thought I was a misfit. An outsider. Instead, I was a trailblazer.

If the math doesn't add up, mustang women don't pretend it does. If the emperor has no clothes, we are the ones who mention that he's naked. We blow whistles when we see injustice. A teacher is mean to your child, and you aren't going to stand for it. Your insurance company rejects a claim, and you appeal it because you know they are banking that you'll get frustrated and quit. You get lousy service from a salesperson, and you dare to say something. We all have lapses when we feel intruded upon and say nothing, but at least we are aware of it and try to honor ourselves enough to push for what is just when we've been pushed too far. We are strong, bold women who behave like wild mustang horses who join and leave their herds at will as they roam free on the range. We'll run with the herd when it takes us where we think we should be going, but we'll split off and travel in another direction if it calls us.

Mustangs Are Bold

As a reporter, I covered Hillary Rodham Clinton's visit to a university campus in Colorado and cringed as a young woman serenaded the then-first lady with a painfully off-key performance. The 5,000 students in attendance ruthlessly booed her until the girl finally quit, saying, "I'm a little too nervous to finish this." But Clinton embraced her, then told everyone, "I have never, except in front of a crowd of two, tried to sing anything a capella in my life. That took class." That young woman who dared to sing off-key was out there, alone, being judged, ridiculed, and misunderstood. Clinton sympathized, because she knew the pain. She's a mustang, too. Name a more publicly skewered mustang than Hillary Rodham Clinton. She's been criticized for her image, her failure to stay home and cook enough cookies, her clothes, her makeup, her politics, her personal decisions, her career path, and her name.

"You didn't even mention my hair," Clinton laughed when I asked about all the criticism she has endured for just being herself. "I have engendered a lot of reaction. Some of it is, frankly, who I am, and I brought it on myself. But, some of it came from the expectations people have about women, what women are supposed to look like, do, say, act, etc."

She hopes other women have learned to deal with this kind of criticism, having watched her stand up for herself. "What I've tried to do—under some pretty challenging circumstances—is just to be able to go to bed every night feeling like I did the best I could do at being me," she said.

She's loved and reviled. Part of the criticism comes because her critics don't want to see a strong woman standing up and fighting. But, part of it comes, she said, from her progressive political agenda. "The kinds of things I believe in or I advocate are, for some people, considered threatening," she said. "It's a real challenge to be yourself. Obviously, that doesn't mean you can be rude or discourteous and get away with ill behavior, but at the end of the day, you have to be satisfied about who you are. Nobody else can live your life. That's what I try to tell myself."

Are we groundbreakers or misfits? Competent women or troublemakers? It's lonely at the top, but, guess what? It's lonely in the middle and at the bottom, too. It's lonely when you stand your ground as your true self, but it's also lonely when you mold yourself into someone who you are not, just to win approval or acceptance.

Martina Navratilova is the most triumphant woman tennis player in history, winning 58 Grand Slam titles. Early on, sports journalists created a rivalry between Navratilova and competitor Chris Evert based on personality and style, not talent. At first, Evert beat Navratilova, who'd defected to the United States from Czechoslovakia. But, as the less-feminine Navratilova got better and began stomping on "Our Chrissy," she was jeered by the crowds. Navratilova remembered the time a sports columnist described their on-court rivalry as a match between good and evil, making her feel like she would always be an outsider. She and Evert played 80 matches over a 15-year period. Ultimately, Navratilova won

43 matches, and Evert won 37. At some point, the fans realized that Navratilova wasn't just a machine, she was a legend. But, she endured plenty of negative press and years of boos before she was appreciated for who she was. "It was the Communists against the capitalists, the lesbian against Chrissy," said Navratilova, whose openness about her sexuality cost her plenty in endorsement money. Over the years, she's stood out front demanding equality for all, regardless of sexual orientation. Navratilova wasn't the type to hold back or tone anything down. "I was always a rebel," she said. "I always did my thing. I knew what I wanted to do and I wasn't going to let anybody tell me otherwise."

She's taken plenty of hits, but she knows she's got to do what she's got to do. So what if she's not "normal," she said. Normal is just a cycle on the washing machine, she added, quoting her friend, singer Naomi Judd. "Do you want to be the mainstream?" Navratilova asked. "I never strived to be average or normal. The mainstream just follows. How can you strive to be there? I was never afraid of leading or speaking out or doing things my way—the way I believed they should be done. At the end of the day, you have to like yourself. You have to like what you see in the mirror. Are you living your life for everyone else, or for yourself?"

Navratilova's in a better position to live larger than most of us. She doesn't have to worry about losing her financial security because of her outspokenness, and there is no boss over her head who might get offended by her behavior. She knows that there are millions of women who don't have those luxuries, but still urges them to find a way to honor their truth without losing their security. "If you have three children at home and the partner is gone, then you have to make a living, and if you have to compromise yourself, do what you have to do, but only for as long as you have to do it. You have to be willing to go for it," she said.

That's the only way to truly live. There are legions of women who feel locked into miserable relationships with the wrong people or endure bad jobs. They live like they have no choice about what they do with their lives, but there is a choice. You don't have to mute your soul or morph into some other persona in order to function in this world. You just have to find the right environment where your brand of boldness is appreciated and encouraged.

Mustangs Are Authentic

You are who you are, so don't give others the power to turn you into something else. Whether you find yourself being challenged to go-along-to-get-along at work, at home, in the community, or in some other place, you will find your center when you remember what it is that made you unique, strong, and passionate in the first place. Tap into that. If you can't be yourself and succeed, you are working for the wrong people. You can use good interpersonal skills, team-building methods, and high-level management training to be more effective in a tough environment, but if you are forced to be a fraud, your success will be way too expensive. We all make compromises to be effective and achieve our goals, but we can't compromise who we are. What a miserable way to win.

As a journalist, I watched one so-eager-to-please editor actually push distorted stories on the front page, rather than tell the big boss his ideas didn't bear out. Once that boss realized she'd damaged the newspaper's credibility, he demoted her. Another editor suffered an emotional breakdown after the 70 hours she put in each week to impress her boss actually convinced him that she was disorganized and ineffective. He demoted her. Another editor suffered repeated public criticism and humiliation by a bullying boss who eventually did promote her because, well, who else would take his crap? Who would want to? All of those women compromised themselves too much, hoping to gain in the long run. In the end, the first two women wound up hurting their careers, and the other sold her soul.

Always go back to your center and your sense of mission. "You have to believe in why you are here," former Environmental Protection Administration Administrator Christine Todd Whitman told me. "Why are you in this position? Think about it. Why are you doing what you are doing? If you believe in what you are doing, then that's what it is all about. Keep your focus on that and don't get thrown off track."

Mustangs Are Distinctive

Sometimes, we have to keep reminding ourselves that all of the emotional and political challenges of being authentic are worth the stress and effort they entail. It can be a lonely, frustrating experience. Caroline Turner experienced this after becoming senior vice president of Coors, breaking the gender barrier and winning what she calls her "seat at King Arthur's table." She was the one woman in a room full of men. "I was an insider," she said. "I had my seat at the table, but I always, *always* felt like an outsider. Did they understand me? No. I think I confused the hell out of them. In that kind of situation, you don't feel lighthearted. You don't feel good about yourself. You feel self-conscious. Your energy is sidetracked into fitting in instead of being good at what you do."

You want to know what has become a bigger challenge than getting that seat at the table these days? It's feeling like we deserve it. It's holding our own, taking charge, and feeling secure enough to be ourselves. Some of America's most powerful women executives admit they walked into their offices at the top with a tremendous amount of self-doubt in tow. That challenge is faced by every woman who dares to stand out, whether she is the boat rocker who upsets the status quo, the woman with the impressive title who undermines herself by questioning whether she's got what it takes, or the woman who stands by herself in a room full of men. It's felt by the woman in management who stands in front of men and women who say they like male bosses better. When we look for the same validation and personhood that we sought as 13-year-old girls struggling at school, we lose our ground and become our own enemies. We've got to appreciate ourselves *because* we stand out. We have fought for and won our chance to sink or swim based on our own merits, but we sometimes find ourselves drowning because of personality clashes and office politics.

"It's like sorority rush," said Yvonne Ralsky, the press secretary at the U.S. Department of Labor. "There is always some group you are trying to break into and trying to win over. I would rather be off to the side a little. I like to float around and do my own thing, but it sure seems like we keep trying out for the cheerleading squad." We blame ourselves when it feels like the squad doesn't want us. We may say or do the same things our male mentors did, but we keep hearing that we are doing it all wrong, coming on too strong, trying to fix things that aren't broken, taking on the wrong issues, pushing an agenda—whatever. Some of us hear a chorus of criticism and gossip, or sense others are waiting for and cheering our downfall.

But things are getting better. Aren't they?

"I wonder if, in a hundred years, they'll be sitting around talking about diversity and someone will say, 'I hired a white male today,' " mused Sally McDonald, a development expert. Most of us assume that the world is getting better—and easier—for women, but sadly, there are

The Basic Principles of Being a Mustang Woman

Become secure with insecurity. You've got the same hang-ups as other women. For example, that extra 10 or 20 pounds or remembering a word of praise for five minutes and criticism for a lifetime. But, your insecurity doesn't hold you back. Despite your flaws, you keep charging forward.

Hold your breath and dive in. No, the rules aren't always clear. Yes, it would be easier to do it the way everyone else does it. No, giving up is not an option. The mustang woman knows how to buck up and win.

Be altruistic. It isn't easy hanging out there by your lonesome, but your sense of mission and purpose will help you through the toughest moments. Really, there is no choice but to do the right thing.

Be passionate. This kind of life sure ain't for sissies. It takes energy, stamina, and commitment. All of that comes from the passion that drives you. You care about what you are doing and who you are. That helps you put up with a lot of grief. It also helps you focus on what matters to you and gives you the creative mind-set to come up with solutions. You live an inspired life.

Be connected. The true mustang woman knows that she's got to build support networks inside and outside of work in order to be as bold as she needs to be. To build better support networks, you have to share the ones you have. Match people who need help with those who can give it, and you'll get help in return. Despite extraordinary odds, resistance, or open hostility, you can get by with a little help from your friends.

some places where it's actually getting tougher." The Government Accounting Office reported in 2002 that 73 percent of all female managers in our country are paid less than their male counterparts. If that doesn't startle you, this might: The numbers were getting worse, not better. Examples? In finance, insurance, and real estate, women managers were paid 68 cents for every dollar men were paid. Five years earlier, they were being paid 76 cents to the dollar. Many women have won their chance to hold mid-level jobs. They can be vice presidents of companies. But only a few will climb any higher. It's still a man's world, even if we don't like to admit it. We comprise nearly 47 percent of the work world, but are just 12 percent of the corporate officers, reported Catalyst, the nation's premier research organization for women and workplace issues. Do men see the inequities? Heck no. Only 13 percent of men said women have to work harder for the same rewards.

Being women, we feel these things deeply. When we don't get a promotion, we assume we don't deserve it. If the good assignment goes to the guy, we figure we weren't good enough. We wonder what we are doing wrong. For Turner, the Coors executive who made it to King Arthur's table, it was like boxing blindfolded. What was she supposed to do to win acceptance in the club? When she told me her CEO would tell her she was "shrill," I asked her if she has ever heard of a man being called "shrill." "Never. Never! Have you ever heard it said that a man has an 'edge'? I can't tell you how many times, during planning or human resource kinds of work, they'd talk about a woman's style and say she has an 'edge' on her. Compared to whom? I would look around the room and see a guy who was a total jerk, yet *she* has an 'edge'? Compared to him, she's a pussycat. But, it didn't fit in that range of what they consider acceptable for women."

Stand up straight and hold your hands four feet apart. That, Turner said, is the range of acceptability for men. It's broad, and stretches from being soft and sensitive on the left side to being a complete jerk on the right. It allows for a full spectrum of behaviors in between. Now hold your hands six inches apart. That is the range of acceptability for a woman. That's her range of acceptable behavior. "If she's over the line on one side, she is too weak," Turner explained, "and if she is on the other side, she is shrill or has an edge." Or, she's a bitch. What is "acceptable" for us? Who the heck knows? Is there a way to deal with the reality of that narrow range of acceptable behavior without sacrificing who we are as individuals? If not, is it so wrong to live outside those definitions?

Some of us have no choice but to push the status quo. We're mustangs, doing what we've got to do in order to make our own tracks. As we start to gain momentum, our presence becomes threatening to other people who want us to stay in our place. We get labeled—often unfairly. Those labels can and do get in our way, said Maryann LaFrance, a professor of psychology and gender studies at Yale. "The first time they see a person as hard-driving and forceful, that is what they assume the person is like in every context, every time, and every place. If they see it twice, it's a done deal, and God forbid you try to do something other than that. People look for verification of views they already hold, rather than disconfirmation. If they are looking for it, they will find it."

Six months after I accepted a job at a Florida newspaper, the managing editor came into our bureau and laid off half the staff. I survived the cut, but reporters who had been there for many years did not. I didn't get it, and asked my bureau chief how they chose who to save and who to spare. "Perception is reality," she finally explained. "It doesn't matter how good you are or how hard you work. What matters is that others perceive you as good and perceive you as hard-working." That is what makes this trailblazing business so tricky. Perception is reality, and perception can kill us when other people don't "get" what we are up to. Our motives may be genuine, but our mission may be so misunderstood or threatening that the only way some people can deal with us is to find a way to distort our objectives or snuff us out. They can be pretty effective.

Look at the legions of women who have left law firms, corporate offices, and other professional jobs in frustration, starting their own businesses where they can just be themselves. One in six women own businesses now. Psychologists say that everything strong women do seems to come out in capital letters. Whether you are causing a flap because you are being too candid or are simply doing a stellar job in a role traditionally held by men, you are an agent of change. Some people will love you, and others will want you to shut up and get out of the way. "If you are an agent of change, you can't look to the status quo for validation because you will never get it. That's why the status quo is the status quo. It doesn't want to change," said Alexa Canady, the first woman and first African American to become a neurosurgeon. "I find white women have a great deal of difficulty with this—much more than black women. They have always been revered, welcomed, and included in everything. The concept of being some place where you are not wanted or included is devastating to them. It is the one time that it is better to be black. When you are pushing your way where people don't necessarily want you, you can't expect that they will be supportive of your goals. Your validation has to come from your family, which is the pattern of Black America because society never did validate us."

Mustangs Are Supportive

I often tell the story of my rivalry with another reporter who used to have a desk right next to mine. When I had a big story, she'd sit there grumbling as editors and other reporters would stop by to compliment my work. When she had a big one, I'd be the one getting jealous. One night, the whole newsroom went to an amusement park after work, and we all got on the bumper cars. Everyone else took turns smashing into bosses, then other reporters, then copy editors and clerks. Not me. I was engaged in a bumper car war with that other reporter, both of us smashing into each other again and again. When I got off the ride, I looked at a friend and said, "This is not mentally healthy behavior. I've got to move my desk." So I moved to the other side of the newsroom and started a new life.

A few weeks later, I had the chance to work on a project and pick a partner. I decided to do something daring and pick my rival. When I asked her to work with me, she agreed. Let me tell you something: the two of us working together on a project made us ten times more effective than either of us working alone. We went to an interview together, and the guy we were questioning didn't have any place to run. When I asked a question, she was thinking of her next one. When she asked one,

I was thinking of mine. It was the most gratifying investigative interview experience I have ever had, and it would never have happened if I hadn't realized that there is real power in turning rivals into partners. The more I have done this, the more I have realized that most of my rivals were other mustangs, and instead of competing against each other, we should have been teaming up.

I cherish a scene painted for me by Alice Rivlin, who served in Bill

Meanwhile Back at the Mustang Corral

Get a group of women friends together and make a point of discussing topics that don't ordinarily come up. Throw the topic out there, and give each woman up to three minutes to talk about it. Afterward, take a few minutes to synthesize what you learned about yourself and each other. Here are some topics that will get the discussion going on your next outing:

During the last 10 years, when have you felt most insecure? What have you done about it? Have your insecurities changed? How much praise do you remember? How much criticism? Do you use your insecurity to make yourself stronger? How? How have your insecurities held you back?

When have you been afraid to do something, but charged forward, re-gardless? How did it feel? How did you rally your strength and keep yourself sane? Who helped you? What did you learn?

What motivates you? If it comes down to mission or money, which wins? How have you changed the world already? Is that important to you? Are there ways you can use your skills to have an even greater impact on society? How? For starters, can you commit to giving 30 minutes to an hour a week to further that cause?

Name five things you have delayed or sacrificed in the last five years. Was it worth it? Were those sacrifices noticed and appreciated? What did you gain or lose from those sacrifices? Would you make the same de-cision again?

Clinton's cabinet as director of the office of management and budget and was the vice-chair of the board of governors of the Federal Reserve System. Her story shows how it is up to us to create our own sisterhood. Clinton's cabinet had a strong nucleus of women at the top, including Rivlin, Donna Shalala, Janet Reno, Madeleine Albright, and others. Although Clinton won praise for appointing many women to key positions, the power center was still all male. Every so often, the women would meet for dinner to share stories, talk about the old boys club at the White House, and—more than anything—connect. "We did count on each other," Rivlin said. "It wasn't to vent. It was to connect."

Our greatest strength as women is our ability to connect. When we are living right, we are doing that with our peers—just as she did with hers. That picture of those legends gathering around the table to connect is the same scene that we live out in our own lives, in restaurants and coffee shops in every part of this country. Despite the struggles we often face, the connections we make will likely be our greatest rewards in life. It took so long for me to learn that you are ten times more effective when you are not acting alone. One time, when Rivlin was taking heat for a position she was taking, Shalala showed up unannounced and said, "C'mon, I'm taking you to lunch." "Women can stick together," Rivlin said. "We supported each other in difficult moments."

UNLESS we live the life of the woman who defers and demurs, we are not going to be universally liked. Even if we know the person who is pestering us is sexist, jealous, inept, or dead wrong, we still walk away uneasy. Studies bear this out. Even when we are certain we are in the right, most of us still feel bad about the flack. We question ourselves. My guess is that this will get easier over time. I look at the battles that police captain Miriam Reed faced as she became the first female division chief at the Denver Police Department, then sued for discrimination when she was demoted for exercising her right to free speech. "Almost every idea that changes the status quo starts out with, 'You've got to be crazy, it will never happen,' " Reed said. "But, if you can last long enough, there is nothing more powerful than an idea whose time has come. Things move from, 'You're crazy,' to, 'We can talk about it, but it won't work,' to, 'I guess we'll give it a trial period, but it won't work,' to, having the trial period and it works well, to the person in power saying, 'It worked well because I proposed this idea a long time ago.' That has happened to so many women over the years. The accolades and recognition go to someone else when other people finally say, 'Why did they do it the wrong way in the first place?' "

✶ ARE YOU A MUSTANG SALLY? ✶

	ABSOLUTELY	PROBABLY	NOT SURE	PROBABLY NOT	NO WAY
A colleague publicly ridicules a very nice, well-meaning, but nerdy co-worker. She doesn't deserve it. Will you tell him to knock it off?	5	4	3	2	1
Your boss is living back in the 1900s and needs to make serious changes if he wants to remain viable. He's very sensitive about criticism and outside interference, but you see big trouble if he doesn't do something. Do you set him straight?	5	4	3	2	1
One of your lunch buddies is suddenly on the "outs" at work because she is too outspoken. The bosses truly hate her and want her to quit. They have been known to judge people by the company they keep. Are you still willing to be seen at her side in public on a regular basis?	5	4	3	2	1

	ABSOLUTELY	PROBABLY	NOT SURE	PROBABLY NOT	NO WAY
You take a management job and realize your employees can't stand you because you are shaking things up. They are somewhat lazy and really need improvement. Despite the need for a major productivity overhaul, will you tone it down so they aren't so put off by you?	1	2	3	4	5
You are in a group meeting and everybody is in love with a project that you know won't work. Do you point out the flaws?	5	4	3	2	1
Someone steals your idea, but you don't say anything because what really matters is that the idea is implemented.	1	2	3	4	5
Your team staged a presentation that you think was just awful. The next day, the group is awash in self-congratulation. Are you going to bring up the negatives or suggest ways things could have been improved?	1	2	3	4	5
You work group is your primary social group.	1	2	3	4	5
Other people remark about how independent you are.	5	4	3	2	1
You are easy to manage.	1	2	3	4	5
You'd rather take no action than make an unpopular decision.	1	2	3	4	5

	ABSOLUTELY	PROBABLY	NOT SURE	PROBABLY NOT	NO WAY
Reading through some old memos, you discover that your boss has done something that is highly unethical—if not illegal. Do you blow the whistle?	5	4	3	2	1
You always wait to get permission or for others to buy into your idea.	1	2	3	4	5
Everybody in your office puts in a ten-hour day. You can get your job done in eight hours. Do you go home when you are done?	5	4	3	2	1
Your friends have planned a girls' weekend, but your husband is giving you a guilt trip for leaving him with the kids. Do you go?	5	4	3	2	1
Someone makes a remark and everybody laughs. You don't get it. Do you laugh anyhow?	1	2	3	4	5
Someone makes a racially insensitive remark. Do you speak up?	5	4	3	2	1
You have to go along to get along, so you make that a priority.	1	2	3	4	5
Your boss makes inappropriate remarks that don't quite qualify as sexual harassment, but do bother you. Do you say anything?	5	4	3	2	1
You are in a bad relationship, but your significant other is going through a tough time and a breakup would be devastating. Do you put off leaving?	1	2	3	4	5

*SCORING

90–100, BRONCO BETTY: You're way out there in the nonconformist zone, and that is likely costing you relationships and opportunities because too much of your my-way-or-the-highway approach is obnoxious and will turn off decent people who would otherwise support you. When you are so rigid in your independence, you've got to expect a lot of controversy, yet you are so far into the nonconformist zone, you don't really care.

80–90, MUSTANG SALLY: You are a mustang. You will generally do what you know is right, even at the cost of friendships, alliances, or political clout. You can be hard to manage, and you'd rather be up front leading, or working on your own. You are not a follower. There are many occasions when you push the status quo, and even though it means there will be consequences, you feel like you have no choice. It's the right thing to do.

65–80, MAINSTREAM MARE: You know that if you stick your neck out too far, you might get your head chopped off. So, you do it—with caution—when you get the courage and the circumstances seem right. You aren't comfortable in the nonconformity zone, but you can deal with it on occasion.

40–65, CONFORMITY COLT: You don't like to make waves, but you will stand up for yourself every now and again. You need to practice asserting and exerting yourself. The more you do it, the more you will become comfortable with standing up for who you are and what you believe.

20–40, PANICKY PONY: You are willing to compromise—way too much. You try so hard to fit in and get along that you will sacrifice pieces of your identity in order to conform. It is clear you like doing what others are doing, and it matters to you that you are a part of the group, not making waves or attracting attention. You'll shortchange your own ideas, success, or happiness in order to make others happy.

A MOMENT OF

ACTION

WITH

Susan Sarandon

*This interview occurred as the Academy Award–winning Susan Saran-
don was under fire for her opposition to the Iraq war. The United
Way of Tampa Bay canceled its women's leadership event because
they thought Sarandon's presence as keynote speaker would be "too
divisive." The same month, Baseball Hall of Fame president, Dale
Petroskey, canceled a* Bull Durham *anniversary celebration because of
the antiwar positions held by Sarandon and longtime partner, Tim
Robbins. Afterward, Petroskey admitted he "should have handled the
matter differently," especially after the Cooperstown shrine was deluged with a reported 28,000 phone calls, letters, and e-mails, the majority of which opposed the snubbing of Sarandon and Robbins.
Sarandon said the experience made her realize how vital it is to speak
up, regardless of the outcry.*

The country I love will cease to be if people can't speak out and ask questions. Then the real damage will have been done. I don't think the United
States would miss me if I never did another movie. I could find lots of
other things that would make me feel whole and bring joy into my life.
But, to have this country lose its civil liberties? That would be tragic.

It's often assumed that people who find themselves taking some kind
of moral stand have some comfort with that decision and feel courageous

and empowered. It's only in hindsight, if it works out, that you are as-
sessed as being brave. While it's happening, that's not the case. But, what
motivates you is the thought of having to live, knowing you were complicit by saying nothing. Most people get to the point where they can't
tolerate the voice inside them that says, "This is not the truth. This is not
acceptable. I can't be complicit anymore by being silent." Really, the
question is, how long can you stand not being who you are, not listening
to that voice inside you?

Everyone has those moments, whether they come while sitting in a
PTA meeting or at lunch where you hear an off-color joke or racial slur
and you find yourself laughing at something you know in your heart of
hearts is not funny. How do you keep that voice alive, the one that tells
you when something really is not right? Our socialization process often
silences that voice. In my case, I have children I am accountable to. At
the end of the day, I want to say that I tried. I did what I could.

There are so many people who come up to me and say, "Thank you.
You are asking the questions we want to ask." For every shock jock who
accuses me in a two-sentence slur about my patriotism, I get a hundred
people coming up saying, "Please, keep speaking out. You speak for all
of us." That takes away from the feeling of isolation.

There has been a co-opting of the language, a redefining of what a
patriot is. If you look at what was used in Nazi Germany, it is always
about fear, and keeping people fearful so they will hand over their rights
in exchange for not getting kicked out of the garden and not participat-
ing. The way it has been set up, it's, please don't participate. That is
where they get you. Their whole strategy is to separate you from the pack
and bring you down. That's why it is so empowering and moving to me
when people write me notes and letters that say, "I have never gone to a
protest before, but I have now."

After the Hall of Fame thing, we got 8,000-plus e-mails thanking us.
After the United Way thing, I got letters from the least likely places. And,
not necessarily from people who agreed with the other issues. They felt
what happened to us was wrong. You see? People are noticing. They are
still awake and they understand that part of living in a democracy is
being able to question. It is ultimately an empowering situation. The

Baseball Hall of Fame incident, for us, was a gift because it really started a dialogue that reassured me that people were watching.

For me, it is easier to take criticism than it is to take praise. I'm just a little embarrassed with the spotlight and with people keeping it on. That is tough for me. I'm very difficult on myself. I'm critical of myself.

Shorten that gap between what you know to be true and honest and actually opening your mouth about it. Looking back on your life, the only thing that will give you any peace at all is knowing you made a difference and did what you know is right.

2.

SUCCESS IS NOT FOR SISSIES

Thriving in Your Discomfort Zone

THE reason I begin this chapter on thriving in the discomfort zone at 4:57 a.m. is this: I woke up in mine at 3:53 a.m. and I could not get back to sleep.

How am I going to finish my book, promote my other book that comes out next month, run my speaking business, take care of my aging parents, and find time for myself? I wondered. *My sales tax revenues are due today. I've got that MRI on my knee at 8:30. I've got to meet with my CPA for my income tax, set up my interview with Carnie Wilson, and get back to the woman hiring me to speak over at Motorola.*

For a moment, I longed for that old job that made me miserable. Predictability! Way back when, I knew I would get a nice paycheck, four weeks of vacation, a good retirement package and great insurance if I could just resign myself to being underutilized and bored. At least then I knew what was coming.

Oh, good grief! Success is not for sissies. If I've learned anything from the women I've interviewed, it is this:

1. No guts, no glory.

2. Expect the obstacles and stay focused on your goals.

3. If you ain't doin' something, you're doin' nothing.

4. If you don't fail a little, you'll never know your limits.

5. You've got to hang in there—especially when it's tough—because you don't know how long it will take to turn the corner.

6. You *will* turn the corner. Tough times don't last forever.

All of those bits of wisdom are especially important when you find yourself in your discomfort zone. Where is that zone? It is that place of uncertainty and unfamiliarity where you find yourself wondering why you had to shake up your status quo. Sometimes, you go to this zone by choice—for example, when moving across country or getting a divorce. Other times, you are forced into the zone because you are laid off at work or betrayed by someone you love. Strong women survive. Bold mustang women learn to see these moments of uncertainty as opportunities to be creative, energetic, and brilliant, and they traverse to the other side of the chaos. There are millions of excuses that make you want to give up or feel lousy, but do you dare to open enough to enjoy the wild ride you are having? If you don't dare to venture into the zone, you'll never know how far you can go or how adventurous your ride can and will be.

Of course, now that it is 5:39 a.m. and I am *still* up writing. I am thinking about how empty some pep talks can sound. It takes a long time to get the perspective that all of these up-and-down, nervous moments are real growth experiences. We all have them. It's how we embrace them that matters.

Embrace your discomfort. When you are afraid, keep moving ahead. Pay attention when your gut is telling you that you are making a mistake, but make sure you aren't scaring yourself out of your own success.

Why Seek Out Discomfort?

Instead of figuring out how to do something, figure out why, said the famed educator Marva Collins. Collins took the $5,000 balance from her pension fund and started her own education program with her own two children and four other youths from the neighborhood. Her story is the legend that led to a movie, *The Marva Collins Story,* featuring Morgan Freeman and Cicely Tyson. Her teaching program evolved into the West-side Preparatory School in Chicago's inner city. Collins accepted learning disabled, troubled children who had been cast off by the system, and by the end of her first year, her students scored five grade levels higher than when they'd started. The kids weren't the problem; the labels and the methods were. Her passion for teaching the "unteachables" evolved into a style that has been modeled all over the world. Of course, when she began, there wasn't much applause.

It all started with Collins's plunge into her discomfort zone. "When I look back on it, it is very frightening. But, I wasn't afraid. It is like I metamorphosed into another person. There are certain things we are born to do," she explained. "You get tired of hearing that you are crazy, but you have to have a strong image of why you do what you do. Average people are always going to try to pull you down because excellence is intimidating to them. Their comfort is threatened. You have to decide if you are out here to be liked, or to be all you can be. Decide what your center is."

Collins has one method that makes the rough moments pass a little easier: she journals. In the moments when she feels unsure or a little down, she grabs a journal that is a couple of years old and reads how she got through a different challenge that was giving her trouble. "I think, *Wow, I got through that. I will get through this.* Sometimes the problem seems too great, but if you have a frame of reference, it's not so bad. I keep thousands and thousands of journals. You get through things one time, and you will do it again." Even if you don't keep a journal, keep a log of some of the obstacles you have faced and overcome. Those will always remind you that you've climbed one mountain and can climb another.

It's also important to try and remember that facing challenges teaches us a lot more about ourselves than we learn by remaining comfortable. One story that struck me as proof was told to me by U.S. Secretary of Labor Elaine Chao, who immigrated to the United States from Taiwan when she was eight. When she left the sheltered environment of her family's traditional Asian home for college, she entered a discomfort zone that was truly terrifying. She'd never even used silverware. While most of her peers at college were partying hard and enjoying their newfound freedom, Chao was trying to make it in a world that was entirely foreign to her.

"Before that time, I'd never even sat down for a full-fledged American-style meal," she said. "At home, we ate with chopsticks. I was new, I was insecure, I didn't understand the college environment. It was the first time I'd left home. I went to my first dinner, and there were all those beautiful blonde girls, and I saw this tray with an array of surgical instruments [silverware] in front of me. It was frightening."

What she learned is that she had a tremendous capacity for adapting in her discomfort zone—something you can develop, too. "Watch other people carefully," she said. "Try not to be too overt in your ignorance. You just watch others, see how they act. Then you learn. You make mistakes, but that's life," she said. "Don't get discouraged. We have an incredibly forgiving society. People have second chances all the time."

Chao said she learned to grow by finding success within herself as she tried new, uncertain challenges. "I have found there's no one way to success," she said. "You have to be yourself. If you're interested, try it. That's what life's journey is all about—learning what you like and what you don't like, what you believe and what you don't believe, what circumstances you will tolerate and what circumstances you won't."

We all have tough moments of adversity when we question whether our risks are worth the anxiety that they bring, but that is all part of growing—a process that shouldn't end just because we have somehow convinced ourselves that we have grown up. "I just want people to know that we have an incredible capacity to change and grow," Chao said. "And if you've had a really bad day, don't give up. The next day is bound to be better."

Thank goodness. Sometimes, one long, bad day is enough. It seemed that way to Meg Whitman, the now famous, visionary CEO of eBay who was at the helm when a 22-hour system crash in 1999 cost her company more than $3 million in revenues and could have cost even more in credibility. People couldn't buy, sell, list, or do business right at the time when the web-based auction forum was making its name. The stock price sunk, especially when another crash happened two months later. In the world of online auctioning, downtime like that is a killer. The press pounced on it, speculating whether the crisis would devastate eBay's preeminence in online auctioning. "Our head of technology was in the Caribbean on vacation," Whitman said. "I spent the next three months sleeping on cots for two nights a week trying to figure out what went wrong." Talk about discomfort.

What did Whitman know about fixing things like that? She was no computer genius. She joined eBay in 1998, when it had 19 employees, was still doing its accounting via QuickBooks, and operated out of a nondescript San Jose office. "I'd give [my high-tech know-how] a two on a scale of one to ten. I was worse than today's elementary school kids," she said. She charged right in, leaving her job running the $600-million-a-year playschool division at Hasbro. Whitman gambled on the power of the human connection that was driving eBay's online auctioning into our everyday lives. Back then, it was a novelty. Today, *everybody* does eBay.

"I learned a long time ago that you just have to ask what you don't know," she said. "So, when I got here, I asked a lot of questions. I'm sure a lot of technology executives thought, *God, she doesn't know a lot,* but when you ask, they want to help you understand." Whitman is heralded as one of the most powerful—and effective—women in the corporate world today. The fact that she has been a woman in male-dominated environments for so much of her career hasn't been offsetting to her, which is something she's talked about with other women who have made it to the top levels. "Most of us have said, 'You know I am a woman, I can't change that, so I am going to try to do the best job I know how to do.' "

Be Comfortable Being "Bad"

Once you step out of the bounds that have been set by the rulemakers, you're going to feel some heat—and discomfort. Stray from that image of being feminine, nurturing, and oh-so-sweet, and, woman, you're going to get flack. Keep moving.

"You have to make a decision in your life. Do you want to be 'good' or do you want to have a life?" asked Eve Ensler, the acclaimed playwright and author of *The Vagina Monologues*. " 'Good' implies being approved of and toeing the line. Living inside a box. Behaving. Having nothing. Being messy. Having everybody love you—which they never do, by the way. It's the suburban world where everything is contained and lovely and you never get your hands dirty and you never live *your* life. You live *their* life." Ensler found her life by traveling around the world by herself. She said it was a time when she felt responsible for every decision

Your Declaration of Independence

Whether you are a mustang Sally or a mustang in training, you may need an occasional reminder that you have chosen this independent path. When you encounter criticism or resistance, center yourself. This isn't the path for sissies, and you can't chicken out now. Write your own Declaration of Independence and keep it where you can get to it when things start getting hairy.

Here's an example:

I'm okay, as is. When my ideas make some people nervous or angry, I keep moving forward because I believe I am doing what is right, and there is really no other choice. Change takes time, and I remember that when I get frustrated or feel defeated. Sometimes, we build bridges for the women coming up behind us, or pave roads that we don't get to drive on. My victory comes with the freedom I have given myself to be who I am, a fun-loving, imperfect, strong woman who sees possibility rather than obstacles, and keeps fighting when others want her to quit. I am who I am, and I like who I grew up to be.

she made. There was no one to blame things on; she couldn't be anyone else's victim or expect someone to come and rescue her. "For women, that is the opposite of everything we have been trained to be," she said.

Ensler believes the hardest thing women have to overcome is their need for approval. Part of the way you learn it is by being rejected, and surviving—getting bad reviews, having people say terrible things about you, and knowing there are people who don't like you, and still surviving. Also, check yourself and know why you are doing something. "If you are doing it for approval, you are doomed," she explained. "If it is for your own soul, politics, and spirit—even if you have to survive the terrible feelings of abandonment by the world—you still have your self intact." Act out. Don't harp on yourself if you are not liked by every single person, or if your actions defy the norm. "I love teenage girls and am spending a lot of time interviewing them right now," Ensler said. "They put their disobedience in their clothing, in their language. Their refusal to be 'good' is all over them, and I find it deeply inspiring because it reminds me that I have to keep that part of me alive all of the time. When you are younger, you find ways to preserve your voice and your dignity. Others see that as acting out."

Just like you, I have wrestled with a need for approval for much of my life. Does this outfit work? Do I look fat? What if I say something stupid? Our self-doubts can cause us to search endlessly for validation and approval, but our brains have the power to take charge and send us onward, despite our doubts. It is okay to wonder about what you are doing and how it is being perceived, because that is one form of feedback that you can incorporate into your perspective. But, don't dog yourself with the negativity and fear that can come by trying endlessly to meet the expectations of others. There comes a point where you have to just do your best for you, then get on with it.

Be Comfortable Being Different

Psychologists refer to us mustangs as "solos." Sometimes we are solos because we are the first women to do something. Sometimes it's because we are the only one doing something. Often we stand out just because we are women in jobs or roles that have traditionally belonged to men, or because we are moving so high up the chain that we are no longer part of the gang. "You can't stand around the water cooler anymore," said Deborah Nelson, Hewlett-Packard's vice president in charge of marketing for all of the Americas. At some point, the isolation kicks in. You know, if everybody is watching you all the time, you start to feel like everybody is watching you all the time. So you make the isolation worse than it is. When it seems like the rest of the world focuses on what you say, how you react, what you weigh, how you keep house, and the way you breathe, you can make yourself paranoid. Plus, you have to deal with all the assumptions that come when people sense that you are a little different. A "little bit out there" becomes exaggerated, and suddenly people think you are *way* out there. If you talk back once or twice, you get the reputation for talking back every time. If you come down hard on an employee once, people assume you are a hard-ass every time.

I was astonished when America's most beloved woman's physician, Christiane Northrup, told me how scared she was when she published her first book, *Women's Bodies, Women's Wisdom,* in 1994. The book introduced new, unconventional approaches to women and their bodies, talking about holistic, natural therapies as well as conventional medicine. Recently, someone told her, "It's hard for me to believe your ideas were ever considered radical." Northrup said she had to laugh. "When I wrote the first book, I thought I would lose my license," she said. "It was terrifying." She remembers waking up one critical night, certain someone was in her house trying to murder her. She started screaming. "I had this moment, a wall of fear I had to walk through. That was the night before my hospital grand rounds meeting—the first time I faced my colleagues since writing the book." What would they say?

"What happened was exactly nothing," said Northrup, an obstetrician/gynecologist who has since become a close personal friend to millions of women who connected to her groundbreaking, mind-body link to all things female. "Nobody cared! They were all living their own lives, going about their own business. Did they talk about me in the operating room? Absolutely. Like most women, I had to get over my fear of not being liked. That is huge for most women, and it was huge for me. But I didn't get killed."

If you want to stand out, you've got to stand up. You can't find your true calling or wildest success by staying in your comfort zone all day, every day, so that means you need to dare to do things that make you uncomfortable and perhaps make other people nervous. It takes a lot of courage to be a mustang, and if you can't handle the heat, the criticism, or the uncertainty, you're not cut out for the ride. People don't achieve extraordinary success by doing things the way they have always been done. When you stray from the norm, those who must have an unchanging comfort zone will resist.

Be Comfortable with the "B" Word

I remember every drunken syllable. "I hear you are a real bitch," an employee slurred to me as I waited in the food line at the company Christmas party. Instead of responding, "Well, I hear you're sloppy and lazy," I internalized everything. What was I doing wrong? I was doing a job, working hard to get results. Why did they think I was a bitch?

I've since interviewed legions of women with their own similar stories and realize the bitch label often comes with the mustang turf.

"You can be liked or respected, but you can't be both. Choose now," Loretta Lynch remembered her boss telling her on her first day at a new job as assistant campaign manager for Attorney General John Van de Kamp's gubernatorial race. "I'd rather be respected," said Lynch. "Great," said the boss. "Go fire this person." That was Lynch's initiation on her first day on the job. The firing put her at odds with the staff for a long time, and the tension remained throughout the campaign. "I know how to use toughness when I need to," Lynch said. "I don't expect to be liked. I've had only female chiefs of staff, and they would visibly cringe when somebody didn't like them. I'd say, 'Why do you expect them all to like you? Do you like everybody?' "

Lynch eventually ascended to being president of California's Public Utilities Commission and led it through its worst days of the rolling blackouts. Her insistence on protecting consumer interests both upstaged and infuriated then-Governor Gray Davis. "I think I got this reputation as a renegade because I was willing to act when no one else would," Lynch said. "To me, it was very clear what the problem was. Once you are clear, then, of course, you have to act the right way. . . . Some people would see me as a bitch, but it was okay to be seen as a bitch. Then they don't step on you as much."

Lynch continued to charge forth until it was reported in the press that Davis replaced her at the helm of the commission because her "maverick streak was said to have annoyed him." A professor was quoted, saying Lynch "was the victim of her own inexperience and hubris."

How Far Will People Go to Obey Authority? Pretty far.

An especially shocking and groundbreaking study into obedience and conformity was done in the 1970s by Harvard psychologist Stanley Milgram, who documented that people would generally do amoral acts— even inflicting great pain on another human being—if ordered by someone who appeared to be in charge. In his experiment, two people were brought into a room, where one, the "learner," was strapped to a chair and attached to electrodes. The other, the "teacher," was taken to an adjoining room and told to ask the "learner" questions. If the wrong answer was given, the "teacher" was told to administer an electrical jolt to the "learner." This started with a 15-volt jolt, but quickly progressed to a serious 450 volts. The "learners" were actually in on the experiments and weren't harmed, but the "teachers" didn't know it was an act. They saw the "learners" screaming in agony, begging for the pain to stop, and in some cases, seeming like they were unconscious or perhaps dead. For the most part, however, they kept jolting the "learners."

Nearly seven out of ten punished the "learners" to the maximum 450 jolts.

The next time you think about blindly following the person in charge, make sure you hang onto your own brain. You know what is right and what is not.

Good God. If a man had been as forceful in accomplishing what she'd done, he'd have been offered up as the next great hope for President of the United States or CEO of General Motors. Instead, they put her head on a block and let the chopper chop. It upset me to see that news article chronicling the demotion, but I thought back to something she'd told me when she was in the midst of the fray: "When you assume you are expected to stand on your own two feet, it's not so scary to take the risk and fail. But you have to be willing to fail and you have to know up front that if it doesn't work out you can walk away with your head held high. You have to do what you believe in."

Strong women leaders are more apt to be misinterpreted and criticized because other people in power are not as comfortable with them, said Bernadine Healy, the mustang who left her job as CEO of the American Red Cross after clashing with her board over how to isolate the donations that were flooding in. That discomfort with strong women will improve over time, but right now it is difficult because women leaders

Mustang Matters

On a night out with your friends, spend a little time talking about life in your discomfort zone. Come armed with one good story about how you had to move beyond your fears and do something that put you *way* out there. When you stepped into your discomfort zone, what kind of reaction were you expecting? What actually happened? Did you get the support you needed? Did you ask for support?

Did you feel like quitting? How did you decide to keep going or stop? How did you energize yourself for another round?

Did that experience make you more or less likely to take a chance again? What did you learn?

Pay attention to the different coping techniques used by your friends, and come up with a group strategy to bolster support the next time one of you mustangs takes a run toward the edge of the cliff. How might you all connect to make things easier? More effective?

Come up with an action plan so you know your army is ready.

are so often criticized for their style as much as for their substance. "They are fair game," Healy said. "A man is described as 'tough' and that is acclaimed. When a woman is described as tough, that is a nasty thing to say about her. And, what do you mean by 'tough'? Tough-mean or tough-minded? Leadership is about being tough-minded, compassionate and tough-minded." And while under fire, it is important that your values and core beliefs about integrity remain steady and "absolutely immutable," she said. Don't run from the heat, she said. "I have never seen objective criticism as heat. I see it as a gift because it forces you to reexamine something you are doing. The world is filled with people who are different types. But, I think the women who tend to get to the top are the ones on the feistier side, willing to stand up, take the heat, and fight for what they believe is right. They are welcoming of healthy debate. I just think that's the way life should be."

Be Comfortable with Your Own Competence

Competence scares people as much as boldness. Mustang women are not going to be universally liked, and sometimes become major targets for sabotage. "Women often get run off," said Lenora Cole, who led the Women's Bureau for the U.S. Department of Labor and was the first African-American vice president of American University. "Actually, it is the more competent ones who do get run off. They get ostracized. They become 'undesirable.' They are regarded as non-team players, and invariably, others will rise up to see what they can do to put them down."

There is a saying, "Only weak men fear strong women." Well, weak women fear us, too. So do some strong men or women who think that they lose something when we win something. Cole said in order to truly succeed, we have to readjust our styles without losing our essence. Readjust my style? Wait a minute! Why should I readjust my style if I am a mustang who lives to be true to myself? Isn't that hypocritical? Learning to be strategic and diplomatic is not destroying the self, but preserving it. Self-preservation is everything if we want to be effective because we have to come to operate in a way that lets us continue to operate. One of my mentors, a woman who is especially adept at survival, reminded me,

"First and foremost, you must survive to fight another day." What good is a mustang who vanishes in her own dust cloud, never to be seen again? This never means selling your soul. It means doing what you've got to do so you can get the job done. Change your approach, change your tactics, but don't change your self.

Competent, powerful women can terrify incompetent or insecure rivals. People who are so set on criticizing or bringing down others who threaten their own standing or progress can resort to being destructive, cruel, and absolutely untrustworthy. So, what do you do when you pose a threat? Just keep on keeping on. "I'm very threatening to people," said Carly Fiorina, CEO of Hewlett-Packard. "So be it. I try not to throw that up in people's faces." I remember being struck by how casually Fiorina wrote that kind of tension off. So. Be. It. All this time, all we've needed to do when we hear others muttering about our being castrating bitches or undermining our work is say, "So? And your point is?"

"If somebody is threatened because somebody is competent, so be it," Fiorina continued. "My experience is that competence will win out. If it doesn't, it isn't worth it."

When you are in the midst of the fray, it's hard to simply wipe your hands and be free of it. It's much easier for men who grew up with the rules of friendly—and unfriendly—engagement as they competed in sports. When the game was over, so was the battle. Most women didn't have that, so we know the aloneness that comes with being "out there." That's why it is so important to bolster yourself with support networks inside your office, inside your profession at large, and outside the office. When you need support, ask for it. When you are in the discomfort zone, say so. Commiserate. You can't protect yourself from everything and everyone, but you *can* insulate yourself from some of the fear and uncertainty by putting good, reliable people around you. And, always be mindful of your role in helping others when they are in their discomfort zones. I will make one point again and again in this book, and that is this: Give support so you'll get support. You don't deserve to get any more than you are willing to give. So, when you see someone else struggling, go help! It may be as simple as saying, "How are you getting along?" Or as difficult as listening to someone venting frustrations for several hours. If you want people to listen to you, then you have to listen to them. If you want people to care about you, you have to care about them. Do it actively, not because you will get something out of it, but because we all will. Find ways to remind yourself to be a good friend and mentor for people when their problems aren't on your radar screen. Train yourself.

One of my mentors, Stephanie Allen, jokes that the word "bitch" really means, "Boys, I'm taking charge here." Maybe we shouldn't take it so personally because it really is the label of first resort by others who are intimidated by our force. Instead of getting lost in all the negativity that can arise when that label is lobbed at us, perhaps we should remember something: hundreds of thousands of truly admirable women have also gotten that label. It's a label. It's not who you are. Keep raising hell.

Be Aware of the Tradeoffs You Make

Almost two years ago, a friend talked me into taking a job as an editor at her publication. My book had just come out and my speaking business was taking off, but I took the job, thinking the security of the paycheck plus benefits would be good for me. Since I'd spent about three years outside the work world to write my book, adjusting to life back in the office was a killer. That first day was the longest day of my life. At 2:27 p.m., I thought to myself, *I'm still here?* The next time I checked the clock, it was 2:36 p.m., then 2:44 p.m. After two torturous weeks, I got the first work paycheck I'd had in nearly three years. I knew, with good behavior, I would receive another in two weeks, then another, and another. Suddenly secure and flush with cash, I felt like I'd been robbed.

I've worked as a journalist since I was 15, but my three-year sabbatical to write insulated me from the challenges most people face by having to get up in the morning and play by someone else's rules. Back in the office, I was feeling that pain again, but it had become a lot more difficult to endure because I'd seen the other side of living. For everything a paycheck gives, it also takes something away. You have money and security, but you don't have the freedom to say, "I don't care what you think. I am doing it my way."

The same week I started that job, I gave a speech to top women executives who had worked hard to earn their six figure salaries. One woman said she was having trouble finding happiness in her life because her job was devouring her soul. I told her it wasn't worth it. She should just pull back and find something fun to do with her life. "You talk about taking risks and doing what matters to your soul," she told me, "but I make a lot of money and I like the comfort it buys me." When it comes to the size of our bank accounts, I told her, you're a lot richer than me. But once you've got your basic survival covered and know that you can make your bills, the amount of happiness that is available to you doesn't change, whether you make $50,000 or $750,000 a year.

The next Saturday, I went sea kayaking on a perfect Florida day in water so calm that I stayed out until the dolphins called me in at sunset. As I paddled toward shore, I stopped to talk to a couple living aboard a sailboat anchored off Longboat Key. Their boat was tired looking and old. They'd paid just $3,000 for it before sailing down from Vermont three months earlier. As we shared the sunset, I remarked that they seemed to be enjoying their boat so much more than the people around them in boats and yachts that had cost hundreds of thousands of dollars. Those people were so busy drinking and making loud talk with their friends that they didn't even notice the changes in the sky.

"They don't get it," I told my new friends on that old sailboat. "It's not about the money." "Not at all," the woman said as she hugged her husband. "We're living on $700 a month. Look where we get to live." I looked at that sky and its reflection in the water and realized I was already the richest woman in the world. So, I quit that job that made me so miserable. It was one of the most important lessons of my life.

Choosing security was my excuse for not betting on myself. It was an out from my dream, from the responsibility to succeed on my terms, doing what I knew I was meant to do. My discomfort zone may give me a few days when I'm not sure of myself, a few mornings when I wake up at 3:53 a.m. wondering how I'm going to pull this off, but living this way, I am who I feel I was meant to be.

Be Comfortable Exploring the Unknown

Although Janet L. Robinson told me she never felt out of sorts with her *huge* life change from elementary school teacher to president and incoming CEO of The New York Times Publishing Company, I know how I'd feel if I were her. I'd feel naked. But Robinson, who loved teaching, was tired of the routine and knew there was more out there for her in the world. She'd always been interested in journalism, and was curious about the business side of the operation. So, she started looking for a job. It took a while to find something where the institutional bias didn't exist and the publication was willing to bring someone in from outside the traditional print journalism framework. *Tennis* magazine hired her. It was owned by the New York Times Company, and it was a great beginning.

"I was very scared, but scared in a good way," Robinson said. "That kind of nervousness can translate into very positive energy. Making a change in lifestyle and occupation at age 33 was a pretty big step. I didn't want to live my life thinking I'd be disappointed I hadn't taken a bigger chance with my life. A lot of people, especially women, put borders on achievement, particularly with regard to age. And, I think 30 is an age where women start to rethink what their future may be. You think, as you grow up, that you're going to get married and have children, particularly by a certain age. And when that doesn't happen, you start scratching your head and saying, 'Is this the kind of life I really want to lead?' And, if I'm not going to find the right person in my life, am I going to live a life that isn't necessarily as fulfilling? Believe me, I thought all of those things."

But, what do you do when you make such a drastic change? How do you make yourself secure when you've just jumped off a cliff and feel like you are racing head first to the rocky bottom below? "Just by realizing that being uncomfortable or nervous or challenged is a very positive thing because it demands the very best of you," Robinson said. "If you're comfortable, you're going to settle for a C performance. That is true whether you're in an academic, business, legal, or political environment. Some things keep you up at night, but once you realize that you are surrounding yourself with smart people and with challenges that are stimulating, that's a wonderful feeling. It's a feeling of exhilaration, and I think if you translate it to exhilaration rather than fear, your performance is affected in a very positive way."

Robinson said we should key in to that inner voice that tells us if we are being sufficiently challenged or need to look for something else to do. Entering the discomfort zone and making change is no easy prospect and may mean more schooling or lower salaries—for awhile. "But, don't be content to be in a job that has no path to where you want to go, because in the long run, you're going to be more miserable than if you'd taken the risk and failed. . . . It's very important not to settle."

Carol Higgins Clark sure didn't. When she graduated college and started acting, her friends wondered why she didn't focus on something more secure. When she started writing, they still wondered about her choice of a profession so far out of the mainstream. Granted, she is the daughter of the mega-selling Mary Higgins Clark, but writing was Carol's calling, too.

"You have to follow your own instinct and your own voice," she

Affirmations to Keep You Moving Forward

I will emerge from this moment stronger, smarter, and even more determined to succeed.

My vision is clear to me now and at all times. I know what I am after and I will myself to succeed.

I approve of what I am doing, I know I am right, and I am moving forward. I validate myself. I feel capable, strong, and sure.

This intensity will die down in time. I can handle it. It'll make for a good story later.

I am growing every minute of this adventure. Success comes from having the courage to take a chance, bet on myself, and live to my potential.

said. "My friends were taking normal jobs, and I was doing what was right for me. It might have looked like I was not doing what was safe, but nothing is safe. You can go to work for a corporation and end up getting laid off. Just do what you really want to do and don't be afraid."

But finding her own voice proved difficult at times, as the daughter of a writer who was already well-known. Carol's first book came out when her mother was just beginning to break out into the super-author strata. It didn't hurt having a mother who was a successful author, but Carol noted, "It would be really hard to start now in her footsteps. Back then she was well-known, but now she is a household word." Comparisons were natural, but Carol's work is very different from her mom's. "I developed my own voice as a writer. I go for the humor; she scares people to death. It was important that I wasn't trying to do what she was doing."

Have the Courage to Fall

Because I always make a mess when I dye my own hair, I usually do it in the bathtub so I get a good soak and my rugs don't end up covered with brown dye stains. One time I was in my bubble-filled tub, dying my hair, talking on the wireless phone, and reading my favorite supermarket tabloid when my 20-year-old cat Chelsea tried to scale the wall of my big tub to see what I was doing. She hurled herself up with a little too much momentum and landed right in the water, making a huge, humiliating splash. She pulled herself from the bubbles, somehow extracting herself from the tub. She leapt down to the floor, swept her little black head back to shake off the excess bubbles, and marched away with as much dignity as any cat could muster, making it look as though she'd planned the whole thing. Cool, reserved, catlike to the end.

I think of that frequently, because I am someone who has had more than her share of uncomfortable, clumsy, absolutely embarrassing moments. Chelsea taught me the value of being a cat when things go afoul. If I trip and fall on a public street or I don't achieve something I set out to do, I just shake it off and keep moving with all my dignity intact. There may be times when you will find yourself falling flat on your face and becoming humiliated, with other people watching. When you dare to jump, there will be times when you don't land as planned. But there will be many, many times when you think you have fallen flat, only to learn the one or two things you need to really succeed.

Most of us have a few battle scars that took years to heal before we could see that they weren't wounds at all. What seemed like a colossal failure was what sparked an enormous success. Just focus on your game. Take hold of those reins, and sometimes loosen them.

"Concentrate on the task at hand," said tennis legend Martina Navratilova. "What is it you are out here to do? I play tennis. I do it very well. Just concentrate on what you have to get done, and the nerves will dissipate. Would you rather be somewhere else? Not really. This is what you have worked for, what you've practiced for. When I am in a tournament, I worked my ass off to get there. That is where I want to be. I want to be there, not on some beach in Acapulco. And, if you don't want to be where you are, you are in the wrong line of work. Rethink."

Like I told you, sissies don't last in the mustang world.

Bernadine Healy knows that as well as anyone. She strongly believes success comes from discomfort. "The things that I have accomplished in my life—the ones that I believe are the most important—are the ones that were the most difficult to achieve and the most controversial at the time," she said. "The most important things that I have done that were lasting and had purpose were not always done easily. They were often subject to criticism and were often things that one of fainter spirit would have walked away from. But, that is not so unusual. Change does not come easily. On the outside, it may look easy, but the road has potholes and pebbles and sometimes major hurdles."

It's hard to twist or turn Healy, and she knows that's one of the problems. When she commits, she stands by her commitment. If she asks someone to do a job, she stands by that person. She expects the same from anybody who asks her to do a job. "But, when the going gets tough, it's not uncommon for the people who said, 'Yes, do it,' to go wobbly. If you have a leader who says, 'I didn't mean that' when the going gets tough, you are not going to have any kind of coherent leadership."

Hear the Voice Inside

One of my favorite editors was a brilliant man with strong opinions. His boss was a not-so-brilliant man who loathed dissent. They clashed. One day, the smart editor came over to me very upset by the fact that his not-so-smart boss didn't respect him. "Why are you so worried about being respected by someone you don't respect?" I asked him. "You know you are smarter. Respect yourself." It's too bad so many of us have trouble doing that.

I've seen many friends put their dreams on hold because they don't want to leave a bad situation until there is some flood of appreciation and warmth from those who do not respect or appreciate them. What happens? Most never leave. If they finally do, their old bosses, husbands, or colleagues rarely have some great awakening about what they have lost. Why wait for respect and appreciation if you can give it to yourself and go on and live for yourself?

Sometimes the most disconcerting, uncomfortable decisions will lead you to a rebirth that is filled with power and reward. The hardest decision, really, is to stay in a situation where you are not fulfilled, happy, or safe. That is a life sentence you don't have to endure. Go for joy.

I finish this chapter almost a week after that last restless night, having awakened from a dream that put me back at work in the newsroom where I was a reporter for eight years. It was a normal day at work, and I had a regular paycheck, four weeks of vacation, tremendous insurance, and a union-protected job that promised me a secure, predictable future. In the dream, my editor asked me questions about my story and she was revved up about it, telling me she wanted to put it on the front page. I had plenty of time before deadline, and I was so used to the job, I could write the story blindfolded.

I was in my comfort zone, and life was so safe, so sure. When my alarm clock went off, I remembered the dream vividly.

It was a nightmare.

A MOMENT OF
EQUALITY
WITH
Nancy Hopkins

*"First I thought it was my problem," said Nancy Hopkins, the molecular biologist and full professor at the Massachusetts Institute of Technology. "Then, I thought it was our problem at MIT. Finally, I found out it was **the** problem." Hopkins's efforts to bring equality to the faculty ranks at MIT not only brought change, but made history. Hers is a story of courage—and connection. Just watch what women can do when they work together.*

I was pretty young when I got tenure—35. On the outside, it looked like I was doing well, but it was extremely difficult to avoid getting trampled. I loved the science, but not the process of what it took to be a scientist. It took me 20 years to realize that the problem wasn't me. The problem was that women were being discriminated against. When they made discoveries, people didn't acknowledge them as equal to the ones men made.

In science, the hardest discovery is the first one, the one that gives you the first insight. I would see a woman make that critical first discovery and some man step in and take over the field. She would disappear. Or, when she made a critical discovery, people didn't talk about it the way they would when a man made a comparable discovery. There was a buzz created around brilliant young men, but not brilliant young women.

I didn't connect the misery I was feeling to how I saw those other women were being treated. When I thought about myself, I thought it was my fault that I wasn't aggressive enough. When I thought about them, I could see they weren't equally valued. It is so hard to believe in discrimination. I thought, *If I really were good enough, this wouldn't be happening to me. If I discovered the structure of DNA, people would be nice to me.* I just kept trying harder and harder. When I saw the other women who were treated badly, I knew it wasn't fair because they were superior to some of these men. But, nobody said anything.

As time went on, I changed the direction of my research and needed some very modest resources. I couldn't get them. I thought, *Wait a minute. I'm a full professor, and if anyone else needed this very small amount of lab space, they'd get it without question.* I had less lab space than the most recently hired assistant professor. A woman who washed glassware in the kitchen said, "How come you have so little space when these men have so much?"

That was it. I couldn't work like that anymore and I was monumentally depressed. I'd have quit if I'd been older, but I went into fighting mode. The dean was the first person who listened to me. I said, "Bob, I'm being discriminated against." He said, "No, you're not." I said, "Yes, I am." He said, "No, you're not." I said, "Yes, I am." But, he did listen to me. He wanted to solve the problem, but couldn't understand what I was saying. Plus, there were tough characters in the system. Male scientists get a lot of grant money and are powerful people in the world of science. It is difficult for an institution to control them.

I wrote a letter to the president of MIT and showed it to a friend who said, "You can't send this. He's going to think you are crazy." I decided to show it to another woman in science. I didn't know her, but her credentials were perfect. People respected her as much as they respected any woman. I wanted her to correct it so it wouldn't be rude or crazy sounding, so I gave her the letter. It was extremely difficult for me to do that because I thought she'd think so badly of me. I thought she would say, "If you were really a good enough scientist, they wouldn't treat you so badly." She got to the bottom of the letter and said, "I would like to sign this letter. I've thought this for a long time."

We became partners in crime, and decided to see whether other women agreed with us. There were 15 women to the 194 men distributed among the six science departments at MIT, plus two women from other departments who had joint appointments. That made 17. The first woman I showed said, "Do you have something to sign? I agree with this completely." One woman said she had no idea what we were talking about, but in the end, she was the only one who didn't sign.

Until all of this, we didn't know each other. We thought we were running into these difficulties because of what *we* were doing, not what others were doing. We wrote a letter to the dean asking if we could form a committee to study it. He said, "When 16 out of 17 women write a letter like this, it has to be true." We got our committee. By the time the committee began its work, we were a bonded group. We knew each others' schedules and we talked every day. I thought of it as the "Summer of Anger." We'd suppressed so much! Everyone was talking, talking, talking. It was quite emotional, very intense, and a *wonderful* experience.

What we found was, the way things worked for junior women at MIT was the same as it had been 20 years earlier: in the beginning, they think the department is supportive, but some time after getting tenure, they feel the support eroding. When they came in at 30 with other men, it seemed like they had support. But, as they aged, the men were moving into positions of power and the women were isolated and marginalized. They weren't on the powerful committees, weren't included in the in-group, weren't able to write grants together, and were doing everything alone. The men were consulting on boards of companies. More than half the women didn't have children and many weren't married. The men were married and had children. These were two different sets of people.

MIT had constantly adjusted salaries to bring people in line, but why did that keep happening? The way the academic system works, people get high salaries by threatening to leave, getting an outside offer, and moving to a different institution. There were women who didn't even know how it worked. When they got a job offer from the outside, they didn't tell anybody. Why would they do that? They wouldn't even think to do that. Some women had even been told, "You are single, you have no children, and I need to get money for the guys who have to support families."

None of us had been activist feminists. We just wanted to be seen as scientists.

The president of the faculty wanted to publish what we found, and the president wrote that he'd always thought discrimination was part perception and part reality. But after reading what we'd written, he realized the problem *was* reality. The *Boston Globe* ran the story on the front page, on the left, above the fold. I think the headline said, "MIT admits bias against women faculty." Two days later, the *New York Times* had it on the front page. Many press articles followed. Two weeks after it came out, I was invited to the White House. It was amazing.

The reaction at MIT was very quiet. There was total silence. Some people didn't speak to me. I think there was a complete belief that it wasn't true. They felt it was hard to believe and they felt guilty and responsible. In time, that changed.

MIT was more extreme in this situation because more than 650 of 950 faculty members are either engineers or scientists, and our numbers are disproportionate with other universities because there are so few humanities, where there are more women. But, if you just looked at engineering and science at other universities, it turned the proportion of women was actually higher at MIT.

First I thought it was my problem. Then I thought it was our problem. Then I found out it was *the* problem. It was a universal problem of women in society.

I got my lab space, my research flourished, I got lots of funding, and I've had an incredibly happy life since this happened. They appointed me to this position to fix this for the university, and placed me on the academic council. That's the highest-level council at MIT. They put me there to help solve this problem. It is astounding. Many women who end up having to sue the institution get killed. For me, I was embraced. It was just a happy, lucky story because we had a wonderful dean and a wonderful president. It took something that could have been a catastrophe and made it a win for everybody.

WELCOME TO MANAGEMENT

Becoming an Effective Leader

"WHY do I scare the hell out of people?" the recently fired female executive asked over dinner, somewhere between the second margarita and the arrival of the quesadillas. She dared to drop the pretense and ask something every woman at that table had wondered, but never voiced. "People either love me or hate me," she said. "What am I doing wrong?"

One by one, the women said that they, too, had spent years wondering what they were doing wrong, why they felt like misfits or outsiders. Their resumes were impressive; not only had they won the titles, but power, too. The trouble was, when they'd exert a little force, things always got ugly. There was always some sort of fire or controversy raging around them. People talked behind their backs, sniping, "Do you know what she's done *this* time?" As managers, they were hired to shake things up, make things better, or improve the bottom line, but when they made changes, many were met with a resounding chorus of, "That bitch!"

Who made these rules? We've got the brains, the guts, and the drive to change the world, but we keep getting told we're doing it all wrong. There are men *and* women who still mumble that they'd rather work for men. People wonder, *Why doesn't she just tone it down, get over it, and play by the rules like everybody else?* Some of us can't. We're mustangs. Some mustangs are born with the ability to know when, how, and with whom to engage. The rest of us have to learn how to play the game. Whether we are mustang women or not, we all need to walk a fine line between standing up for our principles and alienating everyone around us. So how do you lead effectively and still stay true to your own values and beliefs? The strategies in this chapter will help you do just that. Women from former Texas governor Ann Richards to famed Hewlett-Packard CEO Carly Fiorina show how.

Learn the Power of Diplomacy

Welcome to management. Regardless of your title or position, you are a manager. It doesn't matter whether you are the Queen of England or a hot dog seller at the stadium. You are always, always, *always* managing people. Sometimes you do it as the leader, but often you do it in your role as a team player, trying to be effective. The key to effective management: diplomacy. Sometimes, we have to tone down certain things or play up other things in order to get our message heard. In no way does that signify selling out. The challenge is to lead effectively while staying true to our own values and beliefs.

Think about the advantages of communicating with diplomacy, and the disadvantages you face when it is lacking. Manage a waiter or waitress wrong and you might get bad service or, perhaps, be served somebody else's leftovers. Bully your kid's principal and you might make things even tougher for him or her at school. Use the wrong tone with your neighbor and the next thing you know, you're in front of Judge Judy because your dog barked. Be too tough on the volunteers in your organization and suddenly you're not just the president, but the one stuck stuffing envelopes, too. For some people, the concepts of tact and diplomacy are innate, and for others, the art of restraint is completely foreign. It's hard to believe that seemingly innocuous statements can cause resentments that destroy work partnerships or lifelong friendships. The right words at the right time can create an unforgettable moment of goodwill and appreciation. That doesn't mean you should become smiley and fake in order to be heard. It means you need to think about what others want.

According to the legendary former Texas governor Ann Richards, who has quite a reputation for being tough, but diplomatic, you don't have to go along to get along. You do need to get along. "You can find limited success going along," she explained. "But you will never be noticeable. You probably will not rise in an organization because unless you are willing to take risks, you are probably not able to give direction. Leadership requires the desire and ability to direct others." Not all women choose the leadership route, but plenty of mustangs do. "Leaders desperately need followers," she said. "So when I talk to women, I tell them not all of them are going to choose this route, not all of them are going to want to be leaders. And there is a great deal to be said for the workhorses willing to fulfill the role of a follower, and thank God for them. But there is something in our makeup, those of us who are questioners."

Richards contends we mustang women have the ability to be seen in a completely different light. There is a way to avoid the troublesome label of troublemaker. "When everyone is in a room and they say, 'What should we do?' and you speak up, you aren't causing trouble, you are solving problems. The primary result is that you are a problem solver, not a troublemaker. You are a resolver of issues. I really think that's where the creative part of our lives come in—is that we do examine issues and problems and bring a tough perspective."

At the core of good communication are the same practices that make teams click: connection, focus, drive, and responsibility. Many of us aren't used to the nuances of teamwork because so few of us played team sports. It's key to remember that you don't play every position. "You are a part of a team," Richards explained. "It is not necessary for you to know everything because other team members will know pieces you don't. Figure what you have to contribute, then do it to the best of your ability. Never commit to do something that you do not follow through and do. Your word is your bond. Take responsibility. Be known as reliable."

Richards, and others interviewed for this book, also make a practice of not being the first to speak. By waiting, Richard said, "you will hear a lot of things that will probably change what you are going to say. When you are the first to speak, you have the least to add."

Learn to add the little things, just to keep things on a friendly level. Richards suggested you master the art of small talk. "On the weekends when I was working—mostly with men—I would get someone to prep me on what was going on in sports, because almost all meetings with men begin with what is going on in sports. Whether Sammy Sosa hit another home run or Michael Jordan is really going to retire again, you need to be slightly conversant with that world. You don't have to know a lot. Just enough to know what they are talking about. Know how to make a contact. You have to learn to talk about the weather and what's playing at the theater because most people, when they get together, do not go directly to the business at hand. There is a lot of foreplay."

Put Yourself in His or Her Shoes

I was once fixed up with a handsome multimillionaire, the heir to a major bread company fortune. When he asked where I'd like to go, I suggested the most unassuming, inexpensive neighborhood bar and grill that I knew, thinking he'd adore a woman who didn't expect him to impress her with an expensive meal. Surely, he'd want a down-to-earth, blue jeans woman like me who was sincere, intelligent, funny, and not after his cash. He said he'd call, but he never did. We didn't speak the same life language.

Similarly, a new editor took charge where I worked, promising big

> "When I go into a new situation, I always hold back and get the lay of the land and understand what the issues are before I decide how I am going to weigh in on the issue and have people hear me. That's the operative word, hear what I am saying, and not write me off right away based on their assumptions of who I am. Try to create a level playing field where everyone is participating and you are the facilitator. You get the best out of people when they feel you are listening to them and have something to offer. Figure out what their expertise is, so everyone has something they can bring to the table. That has worked for me."
>
> —YOLANDA MOSES, president of the American Association for Higher Education

changes at the paper. You should have seen the brown-nosing and jock-eying that followed. One day, I made a remark about all the insincere flattery he was receiving, and he laughed. Who did he promote? The brown-nosers.

We think everybody thinks and operates in the same world that we do, but that's not the case. They've got their own worlds. We all come to the table with different agendas, beliefs, values, and tactics. Instead of wasting effort trying to get *them* to come around to *us,* we have to go to them. Study who they are and what they want. What motivates and inspires you may completely turn off the person with whom you are dealing. You may be motivated by altruism, he may be turned on by money. You may respond to a promotion, she might rather have an extra week off.

We all think the world revolves around us, but we rarely consider the fact that everybody thinks that. I'll bet you a hundred bucks that 99 percent of the seemingly self-evolved people in this book went straight to the index to look at the pages about themselves first. It's only natural. The last time you saw a group photo that you were in, whose face did you check out first? Then, why is it that you expect people you deal with to see things from the same vantage that you do? They don't, because they aren't you.

> "What you say is not always the most important thing. Your willingness to sit and listen is. Be open and try to learn from every person, whether they are older or younger, because every person has something to teach."
>
> —SALLY PRIESAND, the first woman ordained as a rabbi in the United States

Other people generally aren't worried about *your* goals, needs, and wants. They are worried about *their* goals, needs, and wants. If you are looking for ways to work with them effectively, why not figure out how to make them feel appreciated, and help them get what they want? You've got to travel to the other person's world to see the issue through their eyes. What does he or she want? Why? What is he or she right about? If you were in that position, what would you need in order to feel valued and appreciated? Instead of harping on what divides you, see what unites you, remembering that win-win is always better than win-lose.

When you play win-lose, you win a war, but you also win an enemy. What good is that? Sometimes it takes years to get beyond the post-battle feelings of hurt, anger, rejection, or humiliation. Some people do have that ability to do battle, then go out for beers together, but some people don't. Actually, a lot of people don't. Think about the spats you've had with friends, neighbors, co-workers, and other associates. You probably can't remember everything that has happened, but you can remember enough examples of conflict to prove the point that you might forgive, but not forget. When someone wins something at your expense, there's a possibility you won't forgive *or* forget. If you wind up winning now and paying later, then you haven't won anything. Win-win is so much better than win-lose.

I lead a "Get Real" game during some of my corporate teambuilding

Bear in Mind . . .

You want to get along with others? Here are some human management tips that will work with your loved ones, colleagues, neighbors, and associates:

* Treat others the way they want to be treated.
* Empathize. See their perspectives.
* Be calm, not angry. Get the whole story.
* Pass on positive feedback. Show you value them.
* Stress your availability and your open door, but *you* go to them to keep the dialog going.
* Control your reactions. Think first, then react.
* Find some value in everybody.
* Use the power of humor. It can make fun of catastrophes and help move things forward.
* Let them do their jobs. Don't time their breaks, baby-sit, or micromanage.
* Separate friendship from work.
* Remember they don't have to love working a 60-hour week, offering endless sacrifice or martyrdom, even if you do.

sessions and ask longtime colleagues to share things with each other—for example, parts of their lives that they have never shared. At one government agency, employees who had been together for 10 to 20 years were shocked to find out about some of the activities, feelings, and values that their workmates had. They saw each other as one-dimensional people, defined by their titles or work habits. However, in that group, one woman had lost her son and was still struggling with her grief, another man's wife had taken seriously ill, one woman had been "reborn," and another was studying theology in hopes of becoming an ordained minister. In most cases, these people were spending more time with each other than with their own families, but they had no idea who their colleagues were. How could they motivate and inspire each other if they were strangers?

Rise Above the Fray

Although you need to relate and empathize with others, as a leader you can't get too wrapped up in other's lives and personal dramas. Gossip is soooo interesting, but sometimes you pay a price for even hearing it. Play office politics, but realize they can lead to your own peril.

Janet L. Robinson clings to a simple phrase that helps her if relationships get sticky at The New York Times Publishing Company, where she is president and incoming CEO. She tells herself, "Rise above." "I can only control my own behavior. I think a lot of women have to realize that. We can control our own behavior by rising above difficult environments—not rising to conflict, but making sure we are doing everything we can to lead our businesses the way we should. We have to help people realize they're much better off working in team-spirited environments."

Team-spirited means, not mean-spirited. Robinson said she learned a lot about dealing with others in her previous career, as a teacher. She was constantly evaluating the children, but she couldn't evaluate them in a mean-spirited way. "You are constantly wanting to be their friend in addition to being their mentor, in addition to being their teacher, in addition to being their evaluator. You really have to balance that relationship," she said. Use those same principles in the workplace. "Women leaders have to develop a point of view and a conduct that sends a very clear message when you have to take a different path, or you have to say no, or you have to let someone down. You can do so in such a way that you can retain a wonderful, respectful relationship, but you've also had to make a tough decision. You don't have to be mean-spirited and you don't have to be disliked to be tough."

She's extremely conscious of how she presents herself and she suggests others do the same. "Women should be very concerned about their business reputation—how they speak, how they conduct themselves, what kind of language they use, and their aggressive tactics. All of those things can be misinterpreted. Men can be misinterpreted also, but women more so. Their business conduct can send a very wonderful message about them as women and as executives. Every time you have an interaction with a colleague, with your boss, with someone outside your company, you have to realize that you're constantly making an impression, whether it's the first time or the twentieth," she said.

Tone of voice is very important, she added. There's no reason to raise voices in the work environment. "We all get upset from time to time, but raising your voice doesn't help, whether you're at home raising children or whether you're in the work environment. I think women make big mistakes using inappropriate language and using a tone of voice that is disrespectful of their colleagues. When you do that, you run the risk of losing your professional reputation, and your personal reputation for that matter, and when you've lost it, you've lost it."

> "It's not only what you say, but how closely your actions are aligned with what you are saying. You are not the whole show as the leader, and your understanding of that is reflected in how you treat people, and respect them, their time, and their point of view. One thing I observed is that people who were in positions of power got sucked up to, got indulged, and got spoiled. I observed, very early on, that it must be very hard to stay grounded and humbled in an atmosphere where you are being fawned all over. Leadership is all about effective communication, and one of the challenges is understanding who your audience is, whether it is one to one or one to 1,000. Action trumps words any day."
>
> —BETSY BERNARD, AT&T president

Clearly, her thinking has worked for her, but I can't imagine being that conscious of how others perceive me, or what I say. The same probably goes for several other women interviewed for this book who asked me to edit out the "f" words in their final copy. Maybe we should watch what we say, but, some of us have a little more trouble walking a straight line than others.

Stay Off Their Backs

Try all you want, you aren't perfect and neither is anyone else. Some failures and mistakes actually build self-confidence, said Carly Fiorina, CEO of Hewlett-Packard. One way to improve relationships with others is to stop expecting them to be perfect. Let them win and lose. You've (hopefully) learned from your mistakes, so let them learn from theirs. "I don't think people really gain true empowerment and true self-confidence without having made some mistakes and surviving—picking up and moving on," she said. "I don't know how to tell people how to do that. . . . I think a lot of times people learn more by example than they do by lecture. As a leader, you have to provide opportunities for people to make mistakes and survive. Part of the art of leadership is giving people enough room so they can make a mistake and they can fail, but have it be a small enough mistake and a small enough failure that they can go on."

Always be mindful of the big picture. Will the issue that has you in knots today be important in a month or a year? It's important to not react for the sake of reacting. "I think that frequently, women have too much to prove, so they don't do what I call, 'Stop, look, and listen.' Hold your fire and understand the environment you are dealing with." Fiorina said. "Part of being effective is listening to people, understanding them and communicating in a way they understand. Sometimes that involves softening the blow a little bit or listening instead of talking."

Be Aware of Politics

While you are making it a point to stay off people's backs, be sure to watch your own. Play a situation wrong and you can create a political maelstrom that will impede your path. Fiorina advises women to always remember their larger objective, and like Robinson, urges the importance of remaining removed from the political fray. "Stay focused on making a difference," she explained. "Don't get engaged in a bunch of political conversation and maneuvering that has nothing to do with the essence of business. The essence of business is producing results. The essence of leadership is not only producing results for shareholders and customers, but also about creating more capable organizations and creating an environment where people fulfill their potential. In the end, that is what produces the results for shareowners and customers. That is what it is about. The rest of it will take care of itself, or it isn't of value. I really believe that."

During the interviews for this book, a number of women referred to "big-P politics" and "small-P politics." The big-P politics—elections, campaigns, and that realm—intrigue me. But, the small-P politics have always left me bewildered, stung, and often hurt. "There are politics in everything you do," said Jackie Woods, the executive director of the American Association of University Women. "Anyone who doesn't think there are politics is crazy. There are politics in organizations. In my staff. I need to know what the political obstacles are—if they are real or perceived—and if staff members are playing politics with me. It's like that in

Next Night Out with the Mustangs

Pick one conflict that you would like to fix, and start by looking at the situation from your perspective. Why do you feel the way you do? How strongly do you believe you are right? How important is it for you to be right?

Now review the situation from the perspective of the other people who are involved. What interests do you share? Which are putting you on opposite sides?

Finally, brainstorm some possible resolutions. Come up with at least three, and then decide which one you personally like best, and which would be most palatable to the people with whom you are in conflict. Come up with a compromise that will be acceptable to everyone.

every environment. Small-P and big-P politics are a part of life. You've got to know when to hold and when to fold. Or when to say, 'Excuse me, I need to be at this table.' "

Deal with the politics by remaining focused on your vision, Woods said. "You have to have a goal, a vision, a priority—something that you are striving for. Be clear in your own mind that it is what you want, then articulate it and share it with other leaders and co-leaders in your group. See where your leadership goals intersect with theirs and make sure you are working on the same page. It doesn't mean they are going to do what you want, but it is saying that, yes, this is where you are going." It's proactive leadership that expands your effectiveness with minimal effort. Everyone wants to be valued and heard. Even if you don't follow them, hear them early on. "Anyone who thinks she is going to do it alone or find a way to bring the group along is going to have a harder time. Getting that up-front agreement is important because there may come a time when you have to say, 'We agreed three years ago that these are our five goals. We can change them, but this is what we agreed.' That is how you bring them back home."

Do Unto Others

There is something very sweet about what happened to the editor who assigned one of my reporter friends to do a front-page feature article about a family that spoiled the dog with an air-conditioned doghouse. *He* is now a reporter working for *her*. What goes around, comes around. The lesson is obvious. As a boss, you should remember that the people below you could possibly be your boss one day. As an employee, you should remember that your day is coming. As a human being, if you simply do right by people, you won't have to worry.

People get so hung up on title and position that they lose the very essence of effective communication. We all have dreams and goals. Your goals are as important to you as mine are to me. You want to be treated well by the people above you on the totem pole? Then you'd better treat the ones below you well. You are as good as the next person, and for the most part, the next person is as good as you. So value and take care of people, no matter where they are in the hierarchy. "If you take care of them, they'll take care of you," said Wilma Vaught, retired general of the U.S. Air Force. "There is another part to this. If you don't take care of them, they'll take care of you. I watched people who abused the people who worked for them. They didn't take care of them, didn't work to get them promoted, didn't work to help them, and their people went around them. They got the message to the next echelon of leadership that the person wasn't any good. I saw people get fired from jobs wondering what happened."

People come before paper, Vaught said. If somebody barges in with a problem when you are very busy, you could ask him or her to come back, but he or she might not return. "Take time and find out what that problem is because then you can figure out if it is something you need to take care of right then," she said. "Maybe it is far more important than what you are doing. You might realize you don't need to deal with it right away, but it is so important to be interested in your people."

"When you are in management, there is an invisible line that separates you from those who work for you," Vaught added. Some separation has to exist in order to function effectively. "It doesn't mean you can't be friends, but it means you have got to maintain the separation that makes it possible for you to do something that might be unpleasant. You have to maintain the separation so you don't become part of somebody else's problem. Maintain a distance that enables you to make good, fair judgments. It is just mandatory that you are fair and consistent in what and how you deal with people so they know where they can count on your being. That way, when things come up, they figure out what they are supposed to do, bearing in mind your view on it."

It is more important to deal in the zone of respect rather than friendship. As you learn to negotiate your way through that zone, keep this in mind: at the very core of every person you encounter is that same need for appreciation that you have. Who learns faster and tries harder? The person who is put down or scared, or the one who is encouraged and valued? Whom have you respected more? The person who has respected you, or the person who has demanded your respect? When do you feel like doing something? When you are told to do it because it's your job, or when you are asked to do it as part of the team? Some of this seems like such common sense, but throw in the intensity of the daily grind and some people think they are too busy to worry about kindness or manners. It's a big mistake.

Make Sure They "Get It"

The first time I took a leadership role at work, I had six tasks that needed to be done and six people who needed to do them. Simple enough, right? I divided up our work and went over everything with my committee, spelling out the specifics of who was to do what, and when. Imagine my shock when, on deadline day, only one of the six had done the work! I wondered what the heck was wrong with the others, who just stared blankly when I asked if they'd done their assignments. Had they been on Mars when we'd gone over everything?

Have you ever noticed how many misunderstandings occur when you try to communicate with your husband or significant other? "I meant . . ." "I told you . . ." "Didn't you say . . . ?" Plus, think how many times your words and intentions are misinterpreted by your kids. If things get so messed up at home with the people who know you best, imagine what happens when you go to work and try to communicate your needs and expectations.

"I think at some point, I came to understand that the message I was trying to send wasn't always the message that was being received," said Kathleen Carroll, executive editor of the Associated Press. "You need to do a number of things to make sure, not that people agreed or have been persuaded, but that they understood what you meant. That requires giving it to them a couple of different ways and letting them ask questions so everybody gets a chance to understand.

"Sometimes it means, when you are trying to explain what you are looking for, that you explain what you are *not* looking for. When you ask for something, you can say, 'That doesn't mean I'm telling you to do such and such.' Ask questions like, 'Does that make sense to you? Does that seem clear?' Do that knowing there are people who won't ask questions in public places or knowing there are people who want to sit with things a little before they ask questions."

Pay attention so you can treat people the way they'd want to be treated, and realize that you've got to watch your mouth. "When you realize you have just been short or rude with somebody or somebody says they were worried about something for a whole day, you realize a little of you goes a long way," Carroll said. "I hope I never forget and never lose sight of the power of the job. It doesn't have anything to do with me. I hope I never lose sight of how important it is to be graceful with that, to never seem too busy to talk to people. You need to be seen, be in the departments and in the hallways, and remember to say, 'Thank you,' and 'Nice work.' I don't do enough of that. If I did nothing but that ten hours a day, it wouldn't be enough. But, it's always a goal to say, 'Thank you,' and 'Nice job,' more often."

Move the Team Forward

Imagine being promoted to run a division where every single employee has more experience than you. Welcome to Deb Nelson's world several years ago. How could she manage such experienced people? They knew more than she did, yet she was the boss. In that moment, she defined the essence of leadership. "Working with that and earning credibility with them was a real growth experience," said Nelson, now the vice president in charge of marketing for Hewlett-Packard operations in North, South, and Central America.

> "I was really lucky to have a really bad first boss. Keep a notebook. Remember how it feels. There is nothing better than a bad boss to teach you to be a good boss."
>
> —GERALDINE LAYBOURNE, CEO of Oxygen Network

"Ultimately, I won them over. I knew they knew more than me, so I had to be very clear about where I was going to add value. I was clear that I wasn't going to micromanage them and question every little decision. I trusted them, and trusted that they knew their business. They would teach me parts of it, and my responsibility was to pull the whole team together and make sure the overall business strategy met the needs of the company."

Her previous management challenges had been completely different. In those cases, she was able to put her own team together, and leading was intuitive. This time, she was placed in the job where her staff was already in place. "I had to really think about leading and managing, to make sure I was approaching situations in such a way that the team would be productive and we would ultimately reach our end goal. It wasn't so much that I wanted them to like me, but I wanted them to understand what I brought to the table. I had to think about my approach and how to build that team and be sure we were going to succeed. I wasn't going to take the job and fail."

She's learned plenty of lessons about moving the team forward. For example, you can't be friends with everyone; there has to be a separation between managers and employees. Sometimes, "you have to be a hard-ass," Nelson explained. And, you really never win an argument. "When you win, you lose because you've had it. People carry grudges. Many can forgive, but few forget. I've walked away from a few battles thinking that I've really made my point and won, only to find out that the lingering resentments were far more damaging than the original problem."

When she makes decisions, she does her homework. That means asking plenty of hard questions—something that some people find threatening. "I've been told there are people who are terrified of me. I think that is because I ask a lot of questions," Nelson said. "I peel back the onion. Apparently, that is intimidating to some people." For some, questions seem to be a challenge to their self-worth. They worry whether their answer is good enough, and wonder why you are asking. It's another reminder that there is almost always more going on in a conversation than whatever is being discussed.

Deal with the Jerks

What can you do when you have to work closely with somebody you can't stand? Take a good look at that person. Certainly there must be *something* positive about him or her on which you can connect. Maybe he or she has a good sense of humor, or an appreciation for the same kind of music that you like. Maybe the connection is that you both have children the same age, or that you love golf. As hard as it sometimes is to overlook the huge negatives that a rival or foe may carry, try, try, *try* to find some common ground. You may be right that the person is a jerk, unethical, amoral, incompetent, or something else, but if you have to deal with him or her, stop focusing on how you feel and start strategizing a way to make the relationship work in spite of those bad qualities.

Force yourself to step out of the immediate situation and evaluate it for what is really going on. I am sad to say that I have said, "I'd rather work for a man than a woman" many times in the past. Of course I did! The women I worked for were in no-win situations, being undermined by people above and below them. We all called them bitches, and maybe they were. But they were bitches because of us, and I wish I'd taken a minute to see what they were up against. We expected so much more of them than our male bosses. They had to be competent *and* kind. I had no idea what kind of a high-wire they were dancing on until the moment I crossed into management and had to dance myself. Ever clumsy, I quickly dropped to the ground.

One of my former heroes was an intense, visionary woman who would take on the big boys and shake them down until she'd proved her point. She left meetings drained of energy, sometimes winning but mostly losing. She stayed true to her mission and carried it out with integrity, but it didn't matter how right or competent she was. She'd gotten the reputation for being the girl who ran with sharp scissors who wouldn't do what she was told. I admired her ability to fearlessly push for what she was so sure was right, but she only lasted in her position for a little over a year. When she left her job, she was crushed, bruised, and defeated. At the time, I thought the bad guys had snuffed out a strong female voice. Later on, I realized that, even though her strong female voice was rooted in conviction, it was too strident. Just like mine used to be.

Some people appreciate a hard-charging woman. Some people don't. Some people embrace change if it will make things better. Some won't. Some people find it refreshing when someone tells it like it is. Others find it offensive. I am the last person to tell anyone to "tone things down," but there are times when we have to do exactly that. We aren't any good to anybody if we render ourselves powerless through our stridence. I get e-mails from women every week, wondering why they are being targeted for simply standing firm. The reason is that, despite where we are in our history, there are some men and women who will not let a woman have that firm voice. Even though we should be able to say whatever we need to say, our ultimate goal is to be effective. If we aren't going to change things overnight, we have to step back and use some of the techniques we've looked at in this chapter. Remember what you are after, don't get emotional, and find a way to win the other person over, despite a personality clash. It can be done.

"One rule would be, know what you are talking about," said Alice Rivlin, who served in the Clinton cabinet as director of the Office of Management and Budget and was the vice-chair of the board of governors of the Federal Reserve System. "You have to be competent and informed. You have to have some basis of knowledge before you wade into something. Another is to figure out who can help you get it done. You just keep at it. Sometimes you make the mistakes, sometimes you hire the wrong people, but you learn pretty quickly who you interact with well, who you can trust."

The best preparation for some of these interactions is motherhood, Rivlin said. "I've said that, half in jest," she explained. "It's not entirely facetious. If you spend any time with small children where one says, 'He hit me first!' and the other one says, 'No, *he* hit me first!' you have to get everyone calmed down and distracted by introducing a common project. Public life is often like that. Management is often like that. Women who have managed a family can manage other things because they do have this concept that reducing the conflict and the silly backbiting and the who-did-what-to-whom is necessary, and the way to do it is to get people committed to some common goal and working toward a common objective."

Usually, conflict can be avoided by figuring out everyone's agenda and brokering a compromise, Rivlin added. However, sometimes that doesn't work. "Sometimes, you have to try to win," she said. "One of the strengths of women is that they don't think so much in terms of win-lose.

They think in terms of how do we solve this problem or how do we work together to get it done. Very often, women are better at bringing people together and stopping the squabbling."

Empathize. Empathize. Empathize. Figure out what the other person is thinking about. What is he or she *really* doing? "You can't make consensual decisions on everything, but somebody at the end has to say 'Go,' " said Catherine Morales, vice president of AMS, a major global business and consulting firm. "Ask yourself how what you are saying will affect him or her." Walk in the other person's shoes. If you are talking to clients or other people who are subordinate to you, you have to think about how they perceive you and what you are saying.

When you do have to fix a mistake, don't put it off, advised Sally Priesand, the first woman ordained as a rabbi. "I'm a very diplomatic person. I learned quickly in my career that you have to be able to say you made a mistake, and if you are speaking with a person who is very upset about something, it is easier to say, 'I'm sorry, I was wrong,' " she said. "You take the wind out of their sails. You can move forward and figure out how to fix it. It shows you care. You're not afraid to say you made a mistake and you are willing to listen."

Make Yourself Understood

The one constant lament I hear from bold mustang women is this: "They just don't understand me." It may seem like an oversimplification, but to be understood, you must first understand. As we discussed earlier in this chapter, most people aren't trying to figure out what drives *you* or how true *your* intentions are. They are operating in their own worlds, and they don't take the time to get whatever it is *you* need to get. The best thing you can do is take the steps to enter their realm and understand them.

One of the most revealing conversations I have ever had came when a close male friend explained why he gets so defensive and fights so nasty when someone disagrees with him. "I'm more fragile than you know," he said. "When I feel threatened, it goes straight to my self-esteem. I don't defend myself well."

I was astonished, because I'd always assumed he was just a bully. I wish I'd gone into *his* world and figured out *his* perspective sooner, rather than making so many assumptions about his tactics. Every time I go into a room of extremely well-put-together women who all seem to have good hair days, fine clothes, and great success, I think about how every one of us, put together or not, are unsure of some parts of ourselves. So often, what we say, how we react, and how we are perceived comes down to the same self-esteem issues that honest man owned up to with me.

Why are we so defensive? Why is it so costly to be wrong? Or right? Something comedian and actress Brett Butler said really brings this home. "The times I am quickest to judge and dislike are the times, lately, when I have been pulling myself closer and looking at what is lovable about the unlovable, what is sane in the nuts," she said. "I live in Los Angeles and I see a woman who is surgically mutilated behind the tinted windows of a $150,000 car, and she looks like such a stuck-up bitch. I look closer, and I see a scared little chick."

If we want others to lighten up on us, we need to lighten up on them first.

A MOMENT OF

PERFECTION

WITH

Nadia Comaneci

The perfect 10? Maybe in the eyes of the Olympic judges, and maybe in the eyes of the masses. But, Nadia Comaneci never called herself perfect, even though her 1976 performances led to the first seven perfect 10 scores in Olympic gymnastics history. She thinks she could have done better, making one wonder what perfect really means. The next time Comaneci made huge news was when she left her native Romania in 1989, just weeks before the fall and subsequent execution of dictator Nicolae Ceausescu. She moved to Norman, Oklahoma, to work for gymnastics coach Paul Zert, then reconnected with fellow Olympic gymnast Bart Conner. That's when Comaneci found love.

I didn't feel the pressure to be perfect. I don't think you realize what you are doing when you are young. You finally understand what pressure is all about when you turn 20, not when you are 14. At the time, I didn't even know that I was the first to score a perfect 10 at the Olympics. I knew that 10 in school was the best you could get, and I knew it was the best, but I don't think I quite understood everything that came with it.

I didn't realize that I would be defined by that years later in the history books. People don't care how many medals I won, but they remember that 10.

I didn't feel it was my best execution. Maybe I was a little tough on myself. I don't think perfection is something that can be defined. Maybe I did the best out of everyone who was there, but what is perfection? All our teammates were like sisters, and it didn't matter who was first or second. We never felt that. I wasn't winning all the time. I lost a couple of times, and when I didn't win, it didn't bother me that someone else won. It bothered me that I didn't win because of my mistake. You make mistakes and learn not to make them anymore. If you don't make them, how do you learn?

People had this idea that a kid couldn't take that much pressure. But, what would have happened if I hadn't made it? Nothing. It's not like my parents were going to put me out on the street because I didn't win. Today, the ones to watch are already on the *Sports Illustrated* cover way before the Olympics. There's prediction. There was no prediction for me, so there was no pressure. Everyone was interested in me *after* they saw the 10. Not before.

The Olympics were fun for me. I had fun doing the tricks in the gym, and I'd never experienced the Olympic Village before. I was hanging out with the athletes I'd only seen on the TV. I was hoping I wasn't going to fall down or make a mistake. It was really far away from my country, and I was just hoping my parents would watch it.

I competed in the '80 Olympics in Moscow, but the Americans don't know too much about those games because there was a boycott. It's great when you win, but I went into '80 as the Olympic champion from '76. I knew everyone was expecting me to win, but I didn't win the all-around medal. I was second. I got two gold medals and two silvers, but because everyone was expecting me to win the all-around, they had this idea that, *Oh yeah, you didn't do that well.* But, I got two golds and two silvers. I think that's pretty good! People don't realize how hard it is to actually get the silver.

I always thought it was better to retire in a time when people will regret that you are leaving, rather than to retire in a time when people will say, "Oh my God, is she still around?" It is better for people to miss you. It is good to retire when you are on top.

I do a lot with the Laureus Sports Foundation. Our chair now is [track legend] Edwin Moses. This is an academy that has 40 legends in every sport, and we do nine or ten projects a year for charity. We meet and are sitting at a roundtable. Right across from me is Michael Jordan. To my right is Boris Becker. And, every person accomplished something unbelievable in their life. We want to give something back. Everybody is somebody there. It's hard to describe what it feels like when you are sitting next to those legends: *Oh my God! I'm one of them?*

4.

I Am What I Am

Being True to Yourself

"WHAT do people expect of me?" Janet Reno, the what-you-see-is-what-you-get former U.S. attorney general, mused. " 'Janet, you've got to get smaller glasses.' 'Janet, you've got to get larger glasses.' 'Janet, you've got to get different colored glasses.' 'Janet, you looked perfectly smashing on *Good Morning America* today.' I'll say, 'Thank you. What did I say?' and they'll say, 'Uh, I didn't pay attention.' "

Loved, hated, revered, reviled, Reno. She certainly took the prize for the most publicly skewered woman in federal government during the twentieth century. We loved her because she stood firm and didn't deny where the buck stopped. Her critics wouldn't let her deny where it stopped and always had arrows pointed right at her. In her toughest moments, America's first female attorney general found calm through a relaxation technique that involved her sitting comfortably in a chair, shaking her hands at her side. "Just wiggle, relax, and breathe a deep breath," she said. "I'd say to myself, 'There are things to do in this world. Just do them.'"

In a world full of conformists, you couldn't find a better mustang.

Reno is 6'1", drives a red pickup, and lives without air-conditioning in the Everglades. Back in Washington, she ticked off just about everybody, making decisions that infuriated Republicans (who wanted her to nail the Democrats) and Democrats (who wanted her to stop investigating every twist and turn). Her persona was huge—so huge that *Saturday Night Live* regularly mocked her by hosting the "Janet Reno Dance Party" and the media took shots at everything from how she dressed to why she never married. But Janet Reno never apologized for being Janet Reno. "I flew here from Pennsylvania and I chose my outfit by deciding what was the least wrinkled thing that I had with me. I wash my own dishes. I am who I am," she proclaimed.

When I met Reno, she was in the midst of deflecting a barrage of barbs and ridicule during her unsuccessful campaign for Florida governor. Party leaders publicly groaned to the media about her candidacy, suggesting she just get lost so a more viable candidate could get in and take on Jeb Bush. Reno kept going, connecting with one voter at a time, crisscrossing the state in that red truck and hosting (what brilliance!) a "Janet Reno Dance Party" as a fund-raiser. That's what you'd expect. She's never been known for doing what an angry mass demanded. Remember Waco? Lewinsky? Ellian? The Buddhist Temple investigation? Whether you agreed or disagreed with what she did, you really couldn't dispute that she wasn't afraid to make unpopular decisions and stand by them. She's got guts and is a model nonconformist—very unapologetic about her image, bad jokes, bad polling numbers, and her baggage. "The challenge is to be yourself and not let yourself be shaped into something that you are not," she said, although she admits it can be hard at times. Don't be afraid of your baggage, your wounds, or your defeats, she offered. Baggage just means you've done a few things in your time here on this earth. She's right. At least we've been in there fighting. We can't carry the load without carrying the baggage that comes with it. Staying true to who we are can help during those tough decision-making times when you aren't going to please everybody.

A Level Playing Field?

We've come a long way, but there are many people who still have problems with powerful women. Is there a way to do an end-run around the cultural biases that may limit our effectiveness and still stay true to ourselves? "Our sex is the single most important factor that triggers how people react to us," said former Canadian prime minister Kim Campbell. Campbell, who chairs the Council of Women World Leaders, is also a visiting professor of practice at the John F. Kennedy School of Government at Harvard. "The assumption is that men are competent and women are not," she said. "Women have to prove they are competent. Men do not." That is borne out by fact—lots of it.

What happens when a woman and man who have the same exact qualifications are judged? Study after study has shown that men will rate the man as being more competent. But, guess what? The women will rate the men as more competent, too! This is not whining; it is fact. It's the way our minds make judgments based on patterns or "schemas" that we have internalized, something that Hunter College psychology professor Virginia Valian has so ably documented in her book, *Why So Slow? The Advancement of Women*. When you look at the judgments we each unconsciously make about men and women, you will see why our power is so hard to get and so quickly diluted. "We are all walking around with these beliefs, even if we explicitly disavow them," Valian said.

Here's one study: Five people were asked to sit around a small table, with two on each side and one at the head. Who do you think is the

Celebrating Real Women

Make a list of the ten women you have admired most in your life. What have you admired about them? What made them stand out? Do you have to nurture any of those qualities you liked in them? Is there a way you can learn to embrace the perfectly imperfect part of yourself and better love yourself for who you are—rather than who you aren't?

leader? When subjects were asked that question when all the people at the table were men, they said the leader was the man at the head of the table. When all the people at the table were women, they picked the woman at the head of the table.

But, what happened when the group at the table included both men and women? Well, when a man was sitting at the head of the table, subjects said he was the leader. But when the person at the head of the table was a woman, half of the respondents said the leader was a man who was sitting at the side of the table. Was there any deliberate intention to discriminate? Unlikely. It's just the way minds work with the schemas that exist in society today.

According to Valian, this type of bias means a woman can't count on the same deference that men get. "She may or may not be seen as a leader when men will automatically be assumed to be the leader. She has to work harder to be perceived as the leader," she said.

For example, let's say you start your job the same day as a man who has the same exact qualifications as you, such as same grades, same schooling, same ability. You go into the workplace and do the same job, performing the same quality of work. Much has happened to give us an equal start in the workplace, Valian said, but things quickly become unequal—especially as careers progress. The schemas pile up. One study of "equal" male and female lawyers showed how quickly the man boosts his income through rapid advancement, even though the woman is working as many billable hours and getting the same results.

Every time the question is asked, "Why are there so few women at the top?" we get the same answer: we are in the pipeline, we just haven't had enough time to advance. Well, surprise, that's a lie. The truth is much more subtle. Researchers have found that the pipeline isn't moving us forward all that fast because it is leaking us out. Women aren't listened to or recognized as leaders in the same way men are, so we don't advance like they do. This is proven in study after study, and adds up to something significant. Valian pointed out how frequently a woman will say, "I made this suggestion and nobody paid attention to it. Ten minutes later, Joe made this suggestion and everybody paid attention to it." What happens when a woman brings it up? She's told to stop being so sensitive, to stop making a mountain out of a molehill. "And that is where the accumulation of advantage comes in because it says mountains *are* molehills piled one on top of another," Valian said.

Richard Martell used a computer simulation to prove the point. He and his associates simulated an organization with an eight-tiered hierarchy that was staffed with the same number of women and men at every single level. Then, when giving promotions, it added in a tiny bias that gave men just a 1 percent advantage over women. By the time the staff would have completely turned over, the top was 65 percent male and 35 percent female. "It's the principle that very small changes over time add up to very major changes," Valian said.

Among these schemas, men are "capable of independent action," "do things for a reason" and are " oriented to-the task at hand," while women are nurturing, expressive, and communal. Valian said that this means we see men as acting and women as feeling, which we've heard before. But when we take those judgments into the professional world, it translates into a systematic overrating of men and underrating of women. We're all doing it. Not just the sexist ones. *All of us.* It isn't intentional, either. Valian cites an experiment where male and female subjects were asked to estimate the height of men and women in pictures, which we know translates into some image of power. It should have been easy to tell that the women and men in the photos were the same height because it was obvious. There was always some reference point, like a desk or a door. But, when asked to estimate the height of the people in the pictures, most subjects in the experiment wrote down heights that made the men taller than they were and the women smaller than they were.

When symphonies audition for musicians and the sex of the player is hidden by a screen, twice as many women are chosen, Princeton's Cecilia Rouse with Harvard's Claudia Goldin reported in a study. "When you only hear the music, women get 'better,' " agreed Kim Campbell, the former Canadian prime minister. "The screens screen out the bias, and those who unconsciously—or consciously—assume women play with a 'smaller' technique can't be influenced by perception. If you think women play with small technique, you will hear small technique." The problem is women can't live behind screens, and that means women are often minimized.

That reality may be discouraging, but think of what those studies would have found 30 or 40 years ago. They wouldn't have found much, because it's unlikely anyone would have spent time trying to discern whether women were perceived as anything more than the house cook and maid. In the meantime, we are in place to set the examples that will slowly change those perceptions.

Someone once told Campbell, "You are such a hard worker," to which she responded, "The truth is, I'm really lazy. Thank God I am brilliant." She said women often use powerless speech, asking questions or being way too diffident when making a point ("You might disagree with me, but . . ." "I could be wrong but . . ."). She said she's lost count of the number of women who have told her that, as they have began to assert themselves, they were put down for being arrogant. She's suffered from that description, too. Women are constantly being marginalized by others who say, "Just who does she think she is?" Few of the roughriders I have interviewed have been able to move their agendas without hearing that line again and again.

Win Like a Woman

It *is* tough out there, but there is real beauty in the lessons we learn together as women. We learn them for ourselves and each other. Some tried to play and win like men, and it didn't work. It also wasn't any fun. Women now are learning to embrace the wild hormonal power that really lets us soar.

"We get talked out of our feminine power," said Christiane Northrup, the obstetrician/gynecologist who has revolutionized our view of feminine power in her books. "I have often said that if you want to know where a woman's power is, you have to look to the things that we have been told and taught to be afraid of." Northrup said that includes our period, PMS, labor, breastfeeding and menopause. She recounted the ways women were knocked out or dulled so as not to feel the pain of childbirth as well as urged to feed babies formula rather than breastfeed them. There is so much wisdom and power in our bodies, and we have allowed it to be denied. We've been embarrassed because we bring our feelings to work, but we are women. Our feelings and emotions are not a detriment; they are an asset. It used to be that a woman in menopause was devalued because her prime mission in life—bearing children—was no longer possible. But, look at us now! Most of the women in power are on the brink of or in the throes of menopause.

Northrup referred to menopause as "the mother of all wisdom." "This one we are really taught to be afraid of, because you are a woman who is no longer fertile being thrown on the scrap heap of society—right as your true wisdom ramps up in a *big* way. What is feminine power? It's the power of creativity but in a way of what it takes to birth something and sustain it in the physical world." This means not just babies, but also ideas.

As we grow into our power, there are so many opportunities to use our feminine power. Northrup said that in midlife, so many of us go off and form our own companies and do our own projects. "You can't keep it down," she said. "And, if you don't heed it, your body will speak to you louder and louder and louder. You harness it by knowing the truth of it. You have to acknowledge it." The first thing you do, she said, is notice what you are feeling. Notice when you are tired. Take care of your body. "So the thing about the wisdom is, it is always there, but we keep doing things to stay out of touch with it because if we truly heeded its call we would have to truly change things in our lives." Frankly, that's the most terrifying thing to most people. It's a leap of faith. She added, "Feminine wisdom doesn't offer any guarantees that, if you do this, you'll make a hundred thousand dollars a year. But what it does is say, if you do this, you will be guided to more wisdom and more energy. Your life will be more fulfilling on the deepest level, far more than you ever dreamed possible."

Live In the Now

I was stuck in traffic one hot day in Tampa when a blue classic Corvette Stingray pulled out before me. How cool. Then I got a look at the driver: a woman pushing 80. I suddenly knew who I wanted to be when I grew up. I wanted to be her, a mustang woman to the finish, driving hard and living wild.

It's amazing how much fear we invest in our aging process. I don't like that so many of my friends have been touched by serious illness—actually, it scares me. But the freedom I have in my 40s makes me so powerful and rich. There is no more time wasted on bad choices because I have nothing to prove. All I have to do is just be. It's too bad I didn't learn that in my 30s, but I don't think you appreciate this connection to your true self until you've done your share of stupid things. Now, I just live. I live well, I live now.

I talked with Jane Smith about how much I love my 40s, to which the CEO of Business and Professional Women/USA said, "Fifty is even better. I turned 50 and started flying. Maybe you have never made the amount of money you wanted to make and you never got a MacArthur Foundation grant. Achievers have all these visions of getting whatever. Fifty is a liberation of accepting yourself and your passions and your work around you." She doesn't even answer calls from the people she doesn't want in her life. "When you get to a certain point in your life, the bridges don't even matter. You can burn them." Smith finds living by her principles a more valuable way to live. "My mother died when she was 75, and that was a sign point in my life. I was 50 and I thought, *I wonder if that's my life. If I have 25 more years. If so, how am I going to live them?* Each and every day, I live within my values. I'm productive, and somebody else benefits because I lived that day. If I don't have anything but the length of my mother's life, each day is worth it. I get up in the morning to live a *full* life. I am still in the movement, fighting with a passion to liberate women and blacks, but now my passion is about transferring my knowledge. How can I equip *other* people to continue this campaign?"

Live for Yourself

No, you are not your title, your job. You are your *self*—your family, your home, your friendships, your diversions, your adventures, your hopes, your spiritual self, your career, your agenda, your own complicated list.

"Some people will say, 'I know who I am.' Well, every day, I discover a new facet of me," said the famed educator Marva Collins. "I am 61 years old. The one question I ask my students is, 'Who are you?' I hear Marva Collins and, well, I am a mother and a grandmother and a daughter and a wife, a resident of South Carolina, a teacher, I'm an author and it goes on and on as to who we are. When I write down who I am, I can come up with almost a thousand entities. It's how we think. You are not just Mary Jones. You're courageous, you're perseverant. Once you discover who you are, the more likely you are to keep going."

Her perspective helps us to know our value whether things are going in our favor or not. We are so complex, yet we judge ourselves so harshly when we fall short in one area.

"If you don't know who you are, everything bothers you," Collins said. "I am on a mission. I think life is like a book. You have so many chapters. If you fool around with rereading and procrastinating, you won't get anything done. I am self-motivated, self-generated, and self-propelled. That's why it has worked so well. I am always searching for a better me. Always learning. I always believe in me, even when I am scared to death."

Identity is something you build while you try new things and either

Who Are You?

Leave your title out of this. Come up with 25 facets of the real you, like Marva Collins suggested. Who are you? What defines you beyond your work? Which parts of you do you value most? Which ones would you like to indulge more?

Are you living a life that honors the woman you admire in yourself? If not, why aren't you making changes to bring life to those loves? Instead of losing yourself to the issue of the week, give yourself to the facets of yourself that matter to you.

I'm a cyclist, an outdoorswoman, a hell-raising mustang, a friend. I'm a writer and a daughter and I am living the life I want to live.

Half the challenge of loving yourself is knowing who you really are.

win or lose. Who you are doesn't hinge on the outcome, your title, or your track record. Sometimes you'll win easy, sometimes you'll win hard, sometimes you'll lose in spite of your best efforts. You can't control what happens on the outside, but you can always control who you are, said Yolanda Moses, president of the American Association for Higher Education and the former president of City College of New York. "CEOs of corporations come and go, and there is a certain time for certain people doing certain kinds of work," she said. "You are successful, given the window of time when you are in that position. Earlier or later, it could be different. It is important to understand that to see how much control you have and how much you don't have. How much you blame yourself and how much you don't. It doesn't mean you don't do the same kinds of things, but at least you now know where the pitfalls are." You learn lessons all the time. The lessons build a richer you.

She's learned plenty on her roller coaster. "If you get burned the first time and back away and don't try again, you never move forward. If you do that, how do you grow? It's the process of having those experiences that gives you the opportunities you've earned," she said. "I know where the line is and I know there is life after what I am doing. There are other opportunities. This is not the job that is going to define who I am. It is a part of my life. It is not who I am. I am so much more than this. You have to make time for the other things in your life."

Our identities shift and change throughout our lives, and as we grow, we find meaning in those changes. Actress Brett Butler, who has had fierce battles with sobriety, addiction, and domestic violence, said she's gotten to the point where she realizes that all the trials in her life "almost had to happen. All I know is, it cost me all that to be who I am right now. I'd do it again. I pay a lot of attention to feelings like envy or resentment in my own life. I like to pull those out like bad weeds. Sobriety has taught me that, if there is a trait in someone else that I do not like, many times, it is a trait in myself that I have neglected to work on."

Whoa. That's wisdom. When you can stop pointing fingers at others and take a long look in the mirror, you'll find even greater growth. Don't look for excuses to flog yourself, but make sure you own what you need to own. For Butler, that ownership has led to a peace she never knew.

"I've always put myself in extremely competitive situations because, in competitive situations, that's where people are vying to be the best," Butler said. "I think I'm really good now in noncompetitive arenas, which means being good inside myself and being well-read. That makes my life the coolest kaleidoscope."

The lessons have been profound. Butler married at age 20, and a tempestuous marriage taught her that we have the ability to take charge over our victimization and our past. "The power I have from experiencing the violence is not reexperiencing it daily," she said. "It's knowing that victim is past tense and, in my case, being a victim was a form of a decision I made. It was not fair or right what happened to me, but it was pretty damn stupid that I stayed. When I left, I was stuck with a woman who let this stuff happen to herself. I was just a drunk chick with scars." Making sense of what happened and why gave her a greater sense of self and purpose. She's a far happier person because of it.

The Courage To Be True

The first sentence of the front-page *Denver Post* story said everything. "I was not prepared for the moment a nurse glanced at the digital scale beneath my feet and said, 'Four hundred and sixty pounds for Smith,' " the article began. I knew the author, Kerri Susan Smith, both as a journalist and friend. She'd quit her reporting job to immerse herself full-time at the UCLA Clinical Obesity Center and wrote about her experiences for thousands of readers who cheered her success. The series won awards, was nominated for a Pulitzer prize, and led to a major advance for her planned book, The *Year of Body Transformation*. But, subsequent health battles and life-altering decisions would define her more than any diet or book. In the toughest battles, the real Kerri Smith emerged.

After losing 130 pounds, Smith sold her book. One of the conditions of her contract was that she continue on her successful path, lose another 130 pounds, and weigh 260 pounds when the book was released. It bothered her to have that number in the contract, but she was right on track to make it. Then, she was diagnosed with cancer.

As Smith recovered from her cancer, the hysterectomy, and subse-

quent abdominal surgeries, she strayed from the eating program, quit exercising, broke off her engagement with her fiancé, and moved to
Phoenix. She started gaining weight. The cancer already delayed her
book release by a year, and she then she suffered from lymphedema
which is the accumulation of lymphatic fluid in the tissues that cause
swelling. In Smith, the impairment was so great she couldn't fold her
body in half to sit up. She couldn't stand up to get her shoes on. When I
saw Smith in the hospital, the swelling was so severe, she couldn't bend
her knee. It wasn't fat—it was water, and it was frightening.

The whole time, Smith knew she had to weigh 260 pounds or less
when her book came out. She hadn't shared the extent of her medical
condition with her publisher because she kept thinking she'd get better
and lose the weight. Then it hit her: Even if she could go on a crash diet
and lose the weight, how could she present herself to the world as a
weight-loss success story? She wanted the book to be about the experiences of a morbidly obese person discovering herself and her body. Her
publisher planned to market it as an "I did it, you can, too" book. The
problem was, she hadn't done it.

"One day, I woke up and said, 'I can't do it. I can't. I can just gam-
ble on it and say this is where my weight will be. But, it's wrong to let
this go out with this lie in it. I am concealing what has happened with
this horrific illness.' Everyone wants this chirpy, successful weight loss
book—and so did I—but, it wasn't the truth." She finally made the call
to her agent, who called her editor. The book dream died.

"I had failed at losing weight, again, and this time, I failed publicly.
One colleague said, 'It was heartbreaking to hear of your slide.' That's
how it was perceived. My 'slide.' "

Smith's health battles worsened, and the doctor suggested gastric bypass surgery. Smith had always been skeptical of it, but this time she
knew it was either risk the dangerous operation or die. I just talked to
her—seven weeks post-surgery. She's down fifty-six pounds from 408. A
pair of pants literally slid off of her. The results have been swift and remarkable.

For forty-three years, she has been the same brilliant, beautiful
woman that others are just now starting to see. "People are so much

nicer to me. I look so much more 'acceptable.' I enjoy that, but at the same time, I resent it. I am the same person inside," she said.

Our Moment, Our Rules

We are such fine wine, and always have been. We just didn't realize it. Maybe too many of us have put too much emphasis on one single part of our lives. If that is all we have, we lose perspective when something goes wrong. We think our whole world has unraveled, but it hasn't. "I have this incredible life," said Jane Smith, CEO of BPW/USA. "I have a job, I have friends, I have church, I have family. If one goes wrong, I kick it to the curb so my energy goes to those other things. Your life is made up of so many things. Struggle in one area doesn't reflect your performance in the others."

This is the awakening that we have earned! We have the power to do and dare and be. We have earned the right to define who we are in whatever terms we like. "Age? So, it limits you a little bit." said tennis legend Martina Navratilova. "But, I'm still a hell of a lot better playing tennis than most people in the world. Maybe not as good as I used to be, but does that mean I should not do it at all? I'm still finding new ways to hit the ball. What does it say when I beat somebody who is 23? It says I am one hell of a tennis player. Not that they aren't good, but that I am. I'm still me. That is the double standard. Yeah, I would like to be prettier, sexier. But, that stuff is so inconsequential. I'd rather be who I am and what I am on the inside than be some fake image that is gorgeous who is just trying to blow smoke up everybody's butt and into everybody's eyes. Yeah, I'd have like to have been a little taller, with a smaller nose, bigger boobs, but I'm not going to have surgery. I don't mean to sound egotistical. I like who I am."

Do you?

A MOMENT OF
POSSIBILITY
WITH
Consuelo Castillo Kickbusch

That Consuelo Castillo Kickbusch even went to college or was pro-moted to the rank of lieutenant colonel in the U.S. Army is testament to the power of the American dream. After 20 years in uniform, she retired and took that dream to impoverished children to show that life is filled with possibility. Traveling from school to school, she tells her remarkable story to show that everything is within reach. Just believe and persevere.

My mother was a maid in a hotel. One day, I went to help her and my task was to clean toilets. My mother, who was a perfectionist, tried to make them sparkle. I said, 'Why are you trying to make these toilets sparkle? Some things don't have to be so meticulous.' My mother said, 'Why is it that you think some things don't deserve to be done right and others you can get through by doing them halfway? Whatever work you do, do it right or don't do it at all. While I hope you don't have to clean bathrooms, the standards should be the same, so whatever you do, do it with such quality that you will be known for your work."

She taught me that you have to do your work so well, that when you aren't there, your work will speak for you.

When I went to high school, I didn't realize I was a vocational stu-dent. That meant I wasn't real bright. They gave me general math, general science, and Typing 1 and 2. I was destined to be a secretary. That was the expectation the educators had.

One day, there was a message over the PA system that called for all academic students to report to the cafeteria. I was assuming, because my father taught me I could succeed, that meant me. But, "academic" meant you were taking college preparatory classes. And, as I got in line, my counselor looked at his clipboard and said, "You are not on my list. Where do you live?" I told him and he started to laugh. He pulled me out of the line and said, in Spanish, "Let me tell you something. You know you are like the rest of them. Either get pregnant or marry whoever will have you because your parents will give you to anybody. Go back to your vocational program. Be happy we are training you to be a secretary and don't come back."

I told my dad what happened, and he was shocked. He said, "Why did he say this?" I didn't know. He said, "Then, it is your fault. Because, when somebody tells you that you can't do something, you have to ask, *'Porque no?—why not?'* " He sent me back, and you know, I lived three miles from school, and my dad told me to go back and ask him, "Why not? Why not me?" My counselor looked at me like, "Don't you get it?"

My dad taught me that, as long as I'd work hard, the American Dream was as much mine as anyone else's. He also taught me, "If you cannot give to this country, don't you dare take from it." Of my ten brothers and sisters, eight of us have worn a uniform.

My angel was Mr. Cooper from Laredo Junior College. He said, "Miss Castillo, before I can help you with college, I need to test you and see what your aptitude is. This test is called the Academic College Test— ACT." I took the test and after her got the results he said, "Miss Castillo, are you sure you went to high school?" I said, "Yes, sir, I have my diploma." He said, "I don't know how to say this because the results show you are below average—borderline retarded."

My whole world began crashing. He could see in my eyes that I was the victim of a poor education system. He said, "Listen, I can't give you the college courses. What I'm going to do is put you in a remediation program." So, for a whole year, I was in that program, strengthening my skills. When he retested me, he said, "You are not retarded. In fact, you are above the national average. There is a scholarship waiting for you to go to any university you want." I thought, *This is what my dad said. This is the American Dream.*

I found out there was this little social club called ROTC. I was the only woman and would become the first woman commissioned in Texas. It was 1976. I earned my degree and the dean of student affairs asked my father to give the convocation. I said, "Dean, my father never went to school. He doesn't speak English." He said, "Consuelo, never underestimate what your father accomplished. He was adamant on all ten children having an education." That was one of the most touching moments of my life. I was one of 20 Mexican Americans at this college, and my father was giving the convocation in Spanish. My father cried and we all cried because he said, "I knew this country would be good to my children."

5.

DIFFERENT STROKES FOR
DIFFERENT FOLKS

Embracing Differences in Others

THE first time I took the Myers-Briggs personality test, I called my best friend and said, "This test is easy. The right answers are *so* obvious!" We started laughing because, of course, it is a personality test. There are no right or wrong answers. But that test explained to me why an ultra-anal boss drove me up the wall; an uptight, traditionalist supervisor made me crazy, and a dot-all-the-i's, cross-all-the-t's office manager made me scoot off in the other direction when I'd see her coming.

Turns out, I'm an ENFP: an extroverted, intuitive, feeling, and perceptive type of person.

My "type" suggests I generate ideas and connect well with people. I want to be liked and admired both as an individual and as a humanitarian. I'm a high-energy, unconventional individualist who is outgoing, fun, affectionate, warm, loves people, needs to be the center of attention, hates bureaucracy, challenges tradition. I know, it sounds like quite a personal ad. In fact, if it were, I'm sure I'd turn off as many people as I'd attract. Which is the point. We are all different. We are going to experience intense moments when we feel misunderstood and, perhaps, rejected.

But, that's no reason to feel bad. You aren't me and I'm not you. You can't expect me to think, behave, and feel like you, and I can't expect you to think, behave, and feel like me.

As a manager in the newsroom, I couldn't understand why a third of my employees seemed to just start their stories on deadline, rather than turn them in on time so they could go home. When they were late, they made me late, which made the copy desk have to rush, the layout desk furious, and, if we didn't make up for all the lost time, force the printers into crisis mode and possibly delay the delivery trucks. A late paper costs the company money, and ticks off the readers. Duh. It seems simple enough to just do your work on time and go home, right? I'd always start thinking, *Well, when I was a reporter, I never did that to my editors.* Only now do I realize how disastrous that kind of thinking is. I always turned my copy in early or by deadline because I thought it was professional and, quite honestly, I wanted to go home. Yet, my timeliness was perceived differently by one of my bosses, who apparently preferred to make her home at the office. In her mind, I wasn't giving enough because, unlike her, I didn't want to stay through the night. Why would I? My work was done! Different people, different worlds. Mine was right to me, hers was right to her.

We're all different. There is real power in recognizing and playing to those differences.

Bridging the Disconnect

Alex Sink, who was America's most powerful woman in banking before retiring, explained why recognizing and playing to peoples' differences are so important to leaders. "Motivating people to travel down a certain path is critically important," said Sink. One of the keys to being a good leader is understanding your followers and what motivates them. Different things motivate different people. Some people are motivated by praise, others are motivated by a fear of failure. We can easily be derailed by treating everybody the same way, without understanding that there are many different individual styles and styles of team playing and human management. "You can't sing the same song in the same way to everybody, because people respond in different ways," she said.

"Understanding differences can actually expand your influence," said Claudia Kennedy, the first three-star general in the U.S. Army. "We all come from different perspectives, and between all of us, we'll get the job done. But, if everyone is like me, we will all want to be working on the same part of the same problem," said Kennedy. She recalled a powerful lesson from one training session, when she was given a list of things to take to the moon to establish a colony. She was told to choose 10 of the 50 things on the list. After she finished, she was told to pair up with someone and do it again. Then, they paired with a group of five people. "You learn that a much better outcome is achieved when you have more people working on the problem. They think of different things."

"How well a team works together usually determines success," Ann Richards, the former governor of Texas, said. "You are a part of a team. It is not necessary for you to know everything. Part of the team will know components and pieces, and you should extract what piece of it you can do, and do it well."

If you are trying to lead, think of how you want to be led. You don't want to be dragged into something, you don't want anyone making fun of you for being who you are, and you don't want to be undermined or minimized. You want to be appreciated as an important part of the team because you have your own talents and methods. You are who you are, and you'll do your best when you and those around you are able to perform without second-guessing everything.

"Your job is not to complete your employees," said Kathleen Carroll, executive editor of the Associated Press. "It's not to make up for what they don't have. Your job is to help them identify those things and help lead them to getting more than they need to be complete. Find out what motivates each of them, and give them the pieces of their professional development that are not yet there. The worst thing you can do is create a dependency." She remembers her grandfather telling her about a good boss who was very popular within the ranks. The man dropped dead one day, and while everyone mourned his passing, the work kept going. "That had been his greatest gift to them," Carroll said. "I think that is true. You lead people to find and discover and develop their own gifts and give them the responsibilities for their own careers, rather than taking them on yourself. Don't feel there is only one right answer and only one right place for anybody to be, because you will automatically stagnate yourself and the organization."

Maturing in leadership means understanding how people deal with things their own way. Some people absorb better by reading. Others need to talk things through out loud. Some draw charts and diagrams. Is any one way more right than the other? Of course not. Are you better off having multiple opinions and methods at your disposal? Of course. "You declare what your values are, show people how to have fun with their work, find the smart people in the field who can get it, and take the idea and run with it. And, you reward it," Carroll said. "There is nothing magical about that." And in those situations where you are being led, realize what differences are at play as well. It's all the same lesson: we all have different strengths.

One of the secrets, said eBay CEO Meg Whitman, is knowing what your values and strengths are. "You have to be able to say, 'This is what I do well and this is what I don't do well,'" she said. "And just bring people in on your management team who do what you don't do well. I am not as detail-oriented and process-oriented as would be desirable for a company our size. I have a real clear idea of where we want to go. Let's say we are in San Francisco, and I know we want to go to New York. I know what New York is going to look like, but not how we're going to get there—that we'll need 16,000 gallons of gas, food, or certain people on the bus. I don't have a lot of patience for that level of detail. But, our chief operating officer, that's his strong suit. He's really good at that. My strength tends to be where we are going, and the courage to get the organization focused on the fact that we are going to get there." If you take a few minutes to understand these different worlds—especially if you are a woman with a strong personality—you will save yourself a lot of grief when things don't go your way, or when your way conflicts with others around you.

Mustang women often find themselves in conflict because their types may clash with other types who don't like to see the boat rocked, said Paul Tieger, who has authored five books about personality type with his wife, Barbara Barron-Tieger, including *Do What You Are,* and has trained thousands of managers and human resource professionals. Some conflicts result from the different ways we process information, Tieger said. Thinking types can be a little distant. Feeling types tend to be much warmer, and take things personally. Thinking people are motivated by achievement and success, whereas feeling types are motivated by helping people and being appreciated. The different types are fairly evenly distributed, but nearly 85 percent of all managers are thinking types. Feeling types struggle with management because the dynamics can by disharmonious.

"When the feeling types have to reprimand or discipline or, God forbid, fire someone, they pay a heavy price staying up late at night worrying about it," Tieger said. "Whereas, thinking types are bottom line–oriented. They worry about the bottom line, not the individuals."

This is so important in the business world. Different people are motivated by different things. They react to people in different ways. I cringed while talking with Tieger as he described someone with my personality type walking into a thinking boss's office with the latest creative idea. How is the person who thinks out loud and loves to share ideas going to be perceived by an introverted boss who wants to read proposals and executive summaries, then ponder what he or she is going to do? "He wants specifics about how much time it is going to take, how much money it is going to cost, who is going to do your job while you are doing it, if it is a logical thing to do. He doesn't want to know if it is fun or if it is going to make you happy. Is it good for the company? He wants it presented in an organized way. Make an appointment to talk to him in a week, and do your planning and be there on time."

Uh-oh. I've always been a fountain of ideas, and I've never held back or waited for an appointment. Now I know why I never fit in corporate America. Tieger, who shares my same Myers-Briggs type, told me what my bosses were probably thinking: *Here's that flake, Fawn, coming in with ideas not thought out that she probably had when she had a bite of salad.*

No wonder people in my type tend not to like having bosses. I am fascinated by Tieger's dead-on analysis of what happens when different personalities collide with others who think, feel, and decide in completely different ways. Our personality tendencies work for and against us with different people. You might be a brainstormer who gets juiced up about your creative ideas, but, when the time comes to do sensing things like pay bills, you balk. Work like that might be a challenging and even exciting career to one person, but might wear you out to the point where you feel every bit of energy draining out of your body. Some people like structured environments. Others like all the creative energy and possibility that can exist.

There is plenty to gain by recognizing differences—and playing to them. "Just because I have certain work habits is not to say that everyone that works with me has to have the same habits. You should never set a framework that is written in stone for everyone," said Janet L. Robinson, president and CEO of The New York Times Publishing Company. "We respect diversity in regard to gender and race, so we should

It Took Two Mustangs to Figure It Out

The Myers-Briggs Indicator was written by a real mustang woman, Isabel Briggs Myers, who joined with Mary McCaulley, Ph.D., to found the Center for Applications of Psychological Type. Myers's test brought together the teachings of Carl Jung and research by her mother, Katharine Cook Briggs. For years, Myers's test was practically invisible. But, clinical psychology professor McCaulley found it mentioned in references to Jung's work, so she ordered a copy and immediately saw it for its groundbreaking possibilities. They met in 1964 and started working together.

"I had the credentials to be credible when she didn't," McCaulley said, shortly before her death in 2003. "The chairman of my department said to me, 'Typologies went out in the 1890s. Nobody pays attention to Carl Jung. This woman doesn't even have a Ph.D. Why are you wasting your time?' But, it started catching on, more and more."

Now, the test is used routinely—about 2 million times a year—especially in the corporate world where it is *the* tool for understanding different personalities.

respect diversity in regard to style, and work style may not necessarily mean everyone has to work until midnight every night. Someone may work an eight-hour day and get just as much done. And it may take someone else a little bit longer. You may think that someone is less committed, but in reality, they're not."

Keep remembering: if you expect people to think, react, and behave the way you would, you will be disappointed again and again. It took me a long time to figure that out, although there are still times when I have trouble with others because I expect them to value what I value, to react the way I would react. I value truth, loyalty, and mission. Others may value money, prestige, or a host of other things that don't excite me. I love the work I do, and I've often said that, while I am glad I don't have to do so, I would live in a mobile home just to be able to continue this work. I'm not joking. But, I know plenty of people who would never risk their financial security, even if it meant they could devote their lives to work they truly loved and enjoyed.

When I joke about it, I say I'm in the best Myers-Briggs category, but there truly is no best—only different. Carl Jung, who developed the first three classifications, used to say that we all tend to value our own personality type most. His three classifications, along with a fourth one from Isabel Briggs Myers, have been the basis of personality tests since the mid-1970s. These tests don't measure mental health. They score your personality based on four categories described on the following page.

I talked about the Myers-Briggs test with many power businesswomen in this book and found most were thinking introverts. There are a lot of ISTJs on top. What are you?

What's Your Type?

What are your Myers-Briggs categories? This following simple test, courtesy of Tieger, may help you understand the answer to that question. If you'd like to discover more about your type and learn how that information can be useful to you in many ways, I suggest you visit personality-type.com. To order the actual Myers-Briggs test, visit cpp.com.

1. Are you an extrovert or introvert?

Extroverts (E): They have high energy, talk more than listen, think out loud, and act, then think. They like to be around people a lot, prefer a public role, can sometimes be easily distracted, prefer to do a lot of things at once, and are outgoing and enthusiastic.

Introverts (I): They have quiet energy, listen more than talk, think quietly inside their head, and think, then act. They feel comfortable being alone, prefer to work behind the scenes, have good powers of concentration, prefer to focus on one thing at a time, and are self-contained and reserved.

2. Are you a sensor or intuitive?

Sensors (S): They focus on details and specifics, admire practical solutions, notice details and remember facts, are pragmatic and see what is, and live in the here and now. They trust actual experience, like to use established skills, like step-by-step instructions, and work at a steady pace.

Intuitives (N): They focus on the big picture and possibilities, admire creative ideas, notice anything new or different, are inventive and see what could be and think about future implications. They trust their gut instincts, prefer to learn new skills, like to figure things out for themselves and work in bursts of energy.

3. Are you a thinker or feeler?

Thinkers (T): They make decisions objectively, appear cool and reserved, are most convinced by rational arguments, are honest and direct, value honesty and fairness, take few things personally, tend to see flaws, are motivated by achievement, and argue or debate issues for fun.

Feelers (F): They decide based on their values and feelings, appear warm and friendly, are most convinced by how they feel, are diplomatic and tactful, value harmony and compassion, take many things personally, are quick to compliment others, are motivated by appreciation, and avoid arguments and conflicts.

4. **Are you a judger or perceiver?**

Judgers (J): They make most decisions pretty easily, are serious and conventional, pay attention to time and are prompt, prefer to finish projects, and work first and play later. They want things decided, see the need for most rules, like to make and stick with plans, and find comfort in schedules.

Perceivers (P): They may have difficulty making decisions, are playful and unconventional, are less aware of time and run late, prefer to start projects, and play first and work later. They want to keep their options open, question the need for many rules, like to keep plans flexible, and want the freedom to be spontaneous.

Many companies use these designations and their combinations to help managers better lead their teams. The knowledge that we get our energy, process information, make decisions, and structure our lives differently is profound. Being different doesn't make you right or wrong, better or worse. It's just who you are. And when you don't consider that as you interact with others, you will have problems being understood and appreciated.

Okay, We're Different. Now What?

Maybe the answer isn't in focusing so much on what others do and how they do it, but focusing on how *we* behave in response to them.

Instead of doing what would work with you, try something different, suggested Lucy Gill, a management consultant, coach, and author of *How to Work with Just About Anyone.* "As human beings, we are not creative in the way we deal with problems," Gill said. "We tend to do the same five things over and over. When you are stuck with a difficult person, whether the person is being arrogant or threatening or treating you like you don't matter, take a look at what you are doing in response to it. If you aren't doing anything, you aren't doing something neutral. You are actually feeding the problem." In order to figure out best how to respond, ask the following questions:

1. What is the other person doing that is driving you nuts?

2. What is the problem you are trying to solve?

3. What have you been doing in response to the problem that is not working?

4. How can you go deeper into the puzzle?

Gill, for example, pointed to the stereotypical married couple on television. The wife complains that her husband won't talk to her because he'd rather read the newspaper. She nags him because he is withdrawn, but he is withdrawn because she is nagging him. The more she nags him, the more he withdraws, and around and around they go. Each solution would create more of the problem, not less. When we have a problem with someone's performance, we keep focusing on how to get the other

Back at the Mustang Corral

Next time you and the gang go out to dinner, come with your Myers-Briggs results. If you haven't officially taken the test at work, find one of the free electronic versions available online. If you are feeling especially adventurous, try to look at the different categories and predict where your friends fall on the indicator. Being able to guess well is helpful when you encounter people you don't understand in other environments.

Are you surprised by the results? Spend a little time looking at who is introverted and extroverted, understanding that those indicators don't mean quiet or gregarious. Are your friends "just like you"? And, if they are different, how have you learned to communicate when it comes time to decide what you are doing to make plans? Do friends with like types have some of the same issues you have at home or at work? How have their personality types led you and your friends to success? How have they held you back? Explore the different personality type categories and see if you can guess what category your significant other or your boss falls into. Use this information to better understand why things don't always go as smoothly as you think they should.

person to change. But, if *we* change what *we* are doing, they can't keep doing what they've been doing. We have changed the dance. "If they demand we do the waltz and we hop into a cha-cha, it's hard for them to waltz with us," Gill explained. "We can choose our dance steps, which makes them change theirs."

So, you've got a problem within the ranks. You repeatedly urge a change in behavior, but you are ignored. When you put it in writing, you are ignored, too. E-mails, evaluations—all ignored, too. Same dance step. Change your approach.

Gill cited the example of two different CEOs who assumed their power by ranting, raving, and intimidating the people below them. In the first case, his employee stopped cowering. The employee talked back—in the cartoon voice of Yosemite Sam. After that first flash of humor, the boss didn't yell at him again. The employee had changed the dynamic.

The other CEO was tamed when his employee made an appointment, sat down, and told his very threatening, arrogant boss, "When you yell at me, threaten my job, and come down on me like that, I can't think clearly and my job performance suffers. That's not what I think you want." Gill said the CEO sat there for the longest five seconds of his em-

Changing Your Dance

How might you use Lucy Gill's technique in a situation that has been a problem for you?

1. Ask yourself what is the problem.
2. Figure out what the other person has done that has been an issue for you.
3. Figure out what you have done to make him or her change their behavior.
4. Now, get creative. What can *you* do to change your dance step? Come up with three new approaches, then whittle them down to the one that has the best chance of changing the dynamic that is not working.

ployee's life. "Finally, he said, 'Well, it works on everyone else, but I guess it doesn't work on you.' He never yelled at him or threatened him again."

Gill's point? When what you are doing isn't changing the other person's behavior, change what you are doing. Remember those Chinese handcuffs we used to play with when we were kids? We'd put our fingers in those circular, bamboo tubes, and they'd get stuck. The harder we tried to pull out of the tube, the tighter its grasp. It was natural to pull to get out of the tube, but that wouldn't work. You had to use counterintuitive thinking—push, not pull, and then your fingers would release.

At some point, you have to take your newfound appreciation of differences in style and approach and turn those realizations into action. Pat Mitchell, the president and CEO of PBS, said it all starts with some hardcore listening. Her job—steering the independent leaders of different PBS stations toward a productive vision—isn't easy. "I go through something controversial every week," she said after an especially exhausting week. "I run a pure democracy. Every station has an equal vote. What I do that is beloved by one group of stations is likely to not be nearly as popular or, in fact, not liked at all by another group. It is part of the nature of this particular job. There is never going to be 100 percent consensus, popularity, or approval."

If you're in the hot seat that often, how can you be effective? How can you cater to individual styles, demands, and objectives? "I spent a lot of time listening," she said. "I listened to the things that were wrong and needed to be changed. Once you have given people the dignity of listening and giving them a response, when you take action, it does build some consensus. They feel like they have some role in it. It begins to build teamwork. A second step is delegating, bringing more people into the decision-making process. When a decision is made, you have to stand by it. But, everything is communication. I spend a lot of time making sure everyone is clear about what is going on. I send memos to the station leadership every single week outlining what happened in the week, as well as what is going to happen in the next week. At first, they thought it was a nice gesture. Now it's become a real strategy to get things moving forward."

One thing her people tell her is that she is absolutely clear about what she wants, what she expects, and what she is trying to do. That, she said, is the biggest compliment she can receive. "If you are clear and can communicate clearly, you have set the right tools in place for things to happen."

The Lesson Hits Home

It's one thing when, at work, you can't understand why people are flaky or lazy or sloppy or slow. It's another when you are at home, foisting your expectations on the people you love, and counting on them to do things the way you see them as right and fair. After a spat with your loved one, who is more right: the one who wants to talk the problem through immediately, or the one who wants to withdraw for a couple of hours? What does it say when you carefully choose your words in an argument so you don't offend your partner, but your partner lets 'em rip, not meaning any harm? Maybe you like to cram your weekend with activities from start to finish, but he or she wants to stay at home and read the newspaper. Who is right? You both are. We are all so different in how we view the way things should work in this world. Remember this when you expect others to apologize because you are hurt, or when you don't apologize because you don't think the other person has reason to be upset. Sometimes, it's a matter of perspective. Is it worth losing a relationship with somebody because you are too stubborn or insensitive to appreciate that he or she lives in a different realm than you?

It can be especially difficult when you look at your own child and wonder if you have brought an alien into this world. This is especially true in the years before puberty. How could the same gene pool create such different responses? I remember when my neighbor Penny Noriega explained how different she is from her daughter, Hilary. I love Hilary; she's creative and forceful and daring. But, she's not like her mom or dad, or her older sister. They are all calm, reserved, mathematical, and rule-oriented. Hilary was born a mustang. "She was a drama queen at age two and is still a drama queen," Penny said, affectionately. "That's what makes it difficult, because the rest of us are even-keeled, mathematical-oriented. Hilary is emotional, spontaneous and changes her mind a lot." At first, she and her husband thought of Hilary as "difficult." Then, Hilary's older sister started saying Hilary was the "bad" kid and she was the "good" kid. "But, I really got scared when I heard Hilary talk like she was the bad kid. Most of the family conflicts concerned her not fitting in with the rest of us, and I became concerned that the idea that she was "bad" would become a self-fulfilling prophecy. As a mother, it was up to Penny to figure out how to connect with her daughter, rather than try to change Hilary's essence. Parenting books showed her that Hilary is very extroverted, while Penny is very introverted. What energizes one exhausts the other. "I did not want her growing up thinking she was bad because she was different," Penny said. So, Penny and the family started pointing out Hilary's positives. Hilary is fun, lively, friendly, and outgoing. About a year later, she overheard Hilary explaining to someone that she was the "different" one in the family—and that didn't mean she was bad. She wasn't embarrassed about who she was, and being different was no longer a negative.

As a mother, Penny loved her daughter enough to step into *her* world, and that is the key, whether you are trying to deal with your daughter or anyone else.

A MOMENT OF
SPEED
WITH
Janet Guthrie

In 1978, Janet Guthrie became the first woman to race the Indi-anapolis 500. Because sponsors like male, not female racers, financial support for women on the track is virtually nonexistent. Guthrie's racing career ended abruptly after 11 Indy-level races. Four women who have raced at Indianapolis, and Guthrie raced there twice. En-gine trouble forced her out in 1977, but in 1978, she finished ninth—the best performance of any woman at Indianapolis, so far. No other woman qualified for the race again until 1992. Her helmet and suit hang in the Smithsonian. Guthrie wonders what would have hap-pened if she'd gotten the money to keep racing, and questions why things haven't gotten any better for women racers. Today's most prominent female Indy racer, Sarah Fisher, struggles, just like she did. "I will always wish I had a full season in good equipment," Guthrie said. "No telling what might have happened."

There is an old saying that, when the green flag drops, the bullshit stops. During the 13 years I raced, I could count the problems on the fingers of one hand. The men might have been a little slow to interact, but after the first practice session, when the other drivers saw I could give them some good, clean competition, the atmosphere warmed up considerably.

When I got out of college, I bought myself a Jaguar XK120. The decision was between buying a World War II airplane and the Jaguar. It was seven years old and it was forever breaking down in the most inconvenient places. Professionally, I had a degree in physics and worked as a research and development engineer. It used to worry me why I was doing all those men's things, and finally, I concluded they were the most challenging pursuits that life seemed to offer. In both flying and racing, I was exercising the machinery in an environment where I had to do things right. Otherwise, there could be serious penalties. I liked the challenge.

I think I was just born pushing limits. I had the advantage of growing up in a family where girls were treated the same as the boys. There was never any idea that the boys were going to go to college and the girls weren't.

Racing started out as an avocation and came out an obsession. I raced the Jaguar for five years, then started getting rides in Sebring, Daytona, and other races. I kept sending out proposals for sponsors to the Transom series or others, but finally, I took all of my savings and built a Celica for a professional series that was cancelled before the car hit the tracks. That was a big tragedy.

In the wake of the women's movement, the opportunity came for a woman to drive a car at Indianapolis. I was in the right place at the right time with the right background. I was at the end of my rope financially at that point. I had quit my most recent professional job to race full time so my career in physics was basically gone. I had no savings, no insurance, no rich husband, no jewelry, but I did have a race car and I had this reputation.

I was working on the Celica late one night and got this phone message, "How would you like to test the car for Indianapolis?" I thought, *Yeah, right.* But, I called the key journalist in the business who told me the guy who'd called was legitimate. So, I called him back. I told him that, before I'd agree to race for him, he had to pay for a private test to see whether he liked me, whether the car would go fast enough, and whether or not the situation was viable. The test cost $10,000. If everything passed, I agreed to let him make whatever media noise he wanted. He rented a track for three days and because of problems with the car, I wound up driving another racer's car. My, it was ferocious. What a leap! By the end of the three days, I was turning very respectable lap times and I knew I wanted to go ahead with it.

The attention helped attract more money to my team, so I had money for a better car. I tested it in Ontario. On day two, I was the third fastest driver. On the fourth day, I crashed. The car had been a prototype and it had no replacement parts. Everything had to be built from scratch. The last day, I set the fastest time of the day and made the field. I just knew from looking at my tachometer that my four laps were fast enough to put my car in the field for Indianapolis. That is a moment. It is a moment. The first time any driver qualifies for Indianapolis, it is a moment.

You really have to focus on the details of the sport. I don't know anything as intense as the focus necessary to drive an Indy car. You need to know the nose aspects of all the other cars in the field. That's what you see in the mirror. There is such pleasure in that, in balancing right out there on the edge. There is a certain amount of wildness, but it has to be very controlled. You mustn't endanger anyone else. I can't begin to tell you the immediate post-race euphoria, particularly when you've had a really good race. They pass you, you pass them; it's the greatest fun in the entire world.

A couple of the other drivers maligned my equipment. One of the drivers said, "It's too bad you don't have a better car." Another called it "that shitbox." But, no one told me, "You don't belong here." They said that to other people. The drivers who had sports car racing experience—who had been in the same races where I had a couple of class wins—were willing to take a look at what I did on the racetrack before they said anything. That included A. J. Foyt and Johnny Rutherford. A. J. was probably the first big name who said he'd seen what I had done on the track at Trenton and it looked all right to him. Johnny Rutherford was also very helpful.

I arrived at Indianapolis and, talk about intimidating! I kept telling myself, "This is just like Trenton, only bigger." But, the other side of me was saying, "Are you kidding? This is *Indianapolis!*"

In 1977, I had engine trouble and we finally packed it in and decided the car could not be repaired. I got quite a cheer from the crowd. I waved and said, "I'll be back." I felt certain I wouldn't have any difficulty getting more sponsorships, having accomplished what everyone said was impossible. But, it was tough. I didn't find sponsorship until a month before practice opened. Finally, Texaco came through.

The car I had in 1978 wasn't capable of winning, but I figured that if I gave it a better ride, then it has any right to finish, and maybe I'll get a better ride next time. That's always a tough question. Do you accept a ride in something that's not the best, and make it go faster than it has a right to finish, hoping someone will notice, or do you hold out for something better that might never come?

We had problems in the '78 race. The fuel supply made the fuel go slowly. I'd fractured my right wrist two days earlier, but nevertheless, ended up in the ninth spot. I was very, very pleased and proud of my guys—proud of my team that we'd come together and assembled a successful effort in such a short period of time. That was a good moment. Although frankly, I had hoped to be in the top five and if we hadn't had those problems, we'd have been there. I said, "I have top ten, and I will take it."

We got a lot of media coverage, but it was a question of continuing. Unhappily, Texaco only funded that one race. The car went back to Texaco's possession, and they donated it to the [Indianapolis Motor Speedway] Hall of Fame Museum, where it remains to this day.

After that, I had professional sponsor hunters who predicted it would be easy raising money. But, they worked and worked and worked, without success, and so did I. It didn't happen. In my opinion, male executives don't get that big of a chance to feel macho in their everyday lives and they get a racing team and want a male driver. The female driver doesn't give them the chance to feel macho. I think it is an outrage and a disgrace for the sport that women don't have the funding to continue.

I do wish I had been able to continue, but I wasn't able to because of that lack of sponsorship. I only drove 11 Indy [level] car races, which isn't even a full season, and they were spread out over five years. I will always wish I had a full season in good equipment.

Last night, I had a dream I was back in competition at the Winston Cup, working my way in front of the other drivers. I was competitive. I was right there, not leading, but I was working my way up to the front of a very dense pack. One driver looked over and said, "She's back." You know how dreams are. They are strange.

6.

CHOOSE YOUR BATTLES

Fighting for What Matters

RUMOR had it that Loretta Lynch was sleeping with the president of the California Senate. Five journalists called to ask Lynch, then president of the California Public Utilities Commission, if the rumor was true. It wasn't. But, making matters worse, Lynch started gaining weight because she'd stopped working out in the middle of the chaos. Then word spread that she was pregnant with the man's child.

"They all just believed it!" Lynch recounted, incredulous. "People were offering me seats in committee meetings!" Politics is nasty business—we all know that. But, when *everyone* in the capitol is dead certain that you've stooped as low as a woman can stoop, what can you do? Lynch dealt with the situation brilliantly. "I was furious—for a moment. Then I thought, if that has gone around, then they think I have more influence than I do. I went into a big meeting and they were discussing this proposal. I said, 'I don't know. I can't imagine the senator agreeing to this.' I arched my eyebrow and, without discussion, they abandoned the idea." Lynch is a master mustang. "You have two choices: hide under the bed and quit, or fight. From my perspective, there is too much at stake that needs to be righted," she said.

As tough as it gets, you've got two choices: quit or fight. Anything worth having is going to entail obstacles, and your success depends on how flexible and courageous you allow yourself to be. If you haven't figured this out yet, you will soon. You're not a sissy, so don't act like one! Your battles may be worrisome, scary, nasty, bitter, and hard fought, but they are part of the challenge of standing up for yourself. You're going to encounter detractors, critics, naysayers, and backstabbers. Sometimes there is a way to win them over, sometimes there is a way to neutralize them, and sometimes there is just no getting round them. Keep pushing anyway.

"I know how to use toughness when I need to," Lynch said. "I guess I feel that if I quit or don't stand up for this, they are going to bring someone in who is a whole lot more wimpy. I don't see that there is a choice. I've sometimes felt like a lone wolf in the wilderness, but I absolutely believe in the rightness of my position."

Make the Choice

We've been told a million times that it is important to carefully choose our battles. I *thought* I was doing that, but, as a manager, I always

Choosing Battles

How do you know when to fight or sit one out? Author Sam Horn said, "If it's not that big of a deal, I may not say anything. Especially if it is going to go away." But, she has criteria for choosing battles:

1. Is the matter trivial?
2. Is it a persistent concern?
3. Is the situation innocent or unintentional?
4. What is the background or history of the situation? (Is it your first week on the job, has this been going on ten years?)
5. Can or will it change?
6. Is the timing right?
7. Is it worth the consequences?
8. Will you win the battle and lose the war?

thought I had an obligation to speak up when I saw the team ready to walk off a cliff. Wasn't that my job?

Uh, apparently not. "It's like you are bowling and you see a ball that is destined to be a gutter ball. Sometimes you have to wave at the ball as it rolls toward the gutter and just say, bye-bye. Let it go," said Rosemary Goudreau, editorial page editor for the *Tampa Tribune*. How does she choose which ball to run after and which one to let roll in the gutter? "If it's a matter of my core values—issues of integrity, honesty, or ethics—there are some things you just have to stand up for," Goudreau said. "But

Get Ready to Deal with Your Critics

Look at the people involved. You are the one who knows how people around you react (or don't). Have you thought about their positions? What are they right about? Wrong about? Are they flexible at all? What have they been receptive to in your dealings with them? What have they criticized or rejected? Do they handle criticism well? Are they the types to get even? What kind of mood are they in? (These questions are just for starters.)

Know the subject. What are the five or ten most important facts to support your contention? What are the five or ten biggest weaknesses of your argument? What is the history of the situation? Remember to boil your argument down to three main points. That's about all anyone can digest at one time. When you overload your argument with too many words or too much info, you risk turning the other person completely off.

Figure out your timetable. When do you need an answer? What happens if you delay? What happens if you act too quickly?

Know how much support you have. Who agrees and who doesn't? Do you have the support you need in order to build a viable case? Is there anything left to do to build more support?

Know your motives. Why do you care? You know your position, but where did it come from? Why do you believe in it? Are you being logical? What are you trying to do? Clear the air? Put more information out there?

in the course of every day, there are tensions that don't go to the core. Let some of them go, so that when you speak, your voice will be heard."

There are good reasons to wave bye-bye to that bowling ball, said Alex Sink, the former head of Florida operations for Bank of America, who was the most powerful woman in American banking before retiring. "You have to know when to conform and when to go along, versus when to shake the tree and pick a battle," she said. "There are many, many things you see going in that you don't agree with. You just have to bite your tongue and say, 'This is not my battle. I'm going to speak up when I see something I'm very convinced about, something I am passionate about.' But, it can't be every time because, eventually, you'll get a reputation as being a negative someone who won't go along, won't fit in—somebody who is a troublemaker."

Even when you choose your battles, you might get those judgments, but that's part of a day's ride for a mustang. The need to be liked and approved of certainly causes many people to think twice before going into battle, but trailblazers know that sometimes they have to charge forward, regardless. Bernadine Healy, a controversial, historic woman, put it all in perspective. "If your goal in life is to have everybody like you, you will never do anything. You will never stand up for anything, make any commitment, or figure out what you believe in because you will be afraid it will be offensive to everybody else," she said. And she should know: She is the person who put women's health on the map when she ran the National Institutes of Health. She also made big news when she abruptly retired as executive director of the American Red Cross because she clashed with the organization's board about how donations following the 9-11 disasters would be spent. "You want people to like you for the right reasons, not for some veneer you put on," she explained. "It doesn't mean they have to agree with what you do. You hope the ones who like you will say, 'I don't think you are doing this right,' and say it in a constructive and caring way."

I saw Healy at an event a few days after her resignation from the American Red Cross. News stories described her as "embattled" and "beleaguered," and I felt for her because I'd had my own moments of being embattled and beleaguered, as well. But there was a resolve in her eyes that I will never forget. Despite the pain that comes with standing up and potentially being shot down, there is a reward in being true to yourself. Healy, for example, now serves on the President's Council of Advisors of Science.

Remember, when something burns inside of you, find the courage to say what needs to be said and fight the battle you must fight. Some people hesitate because they fear they'll make enemies. It isn't about the enemies. It's about a truth that you will constantly confront throughout your life. When Patty Ivey, a construction project engineer, found herself being sabotaged at work, she discovered there was this "untapped beast inside me," she said. Ivey worked as a woman in a man's world and encountered a steady dose of jealousy and resentment as she won honors for her work. Ivey fought back, filing formal grievances that pushed her to push her limits. "I had always been somewhat shy in asserting my position, and would consequently go along with the status quo. However, when it came to personal and professional ethics, there was a fire that just erupted in me. Drawing a line in the sand and sticking by it is difficult when you're being bullied from all sides. But that fire—that passion—absolutely fuels the ability to have the courage to say what you feel, and to not second-guess or feel guilty about your position."

A friend rehearsed and coached her as she braced for the repeated clashes that tested whether she was up to the fight. "My friend made me go through a role-playing routine," she said. "We went over it, and over it, and over it some more. There's a fakeness to role-playing because, after all, it *is* acting, and I wasn't real comfortable with that. I was embarrassed for her to see how tongue-tied I could get." But, with practice, it got easier. It prepared her for dealing with her saboteurs. When it was all over, she won her grievances and the others were disciplined. "I couldn't believe I pulled it off! It was *so* worth it. What a confidence builder. No one likes conflict, but if you meet it head on, with confidence and the power of your convictions, it becomes second nature."

Seize the Moment

No wonder we are always caught off guard and kicking ourselves because we blew a chance to say the right thing. Maybe we just need to practice. I just had lunch with a friend who is about to quit her job and start her own business. She worried that her boss might grumble about unfinished projects or say mean things to her when she announced her resignation. "Let's role-play," I said. "You be him and I will be you." So, she started complaining about projects that weren't done and I said, "Now, Nick, I know you mean to be saying, 'Congratulations are in order! Good luck, Kathy!'" She stayed in character and started grumbling again, but I waved my hand in front of her mouth. "Ooooooh, Nick, I know you mean to be supportive and wish me well," giving her a rather humorous and unexpected way out if things got rough. We usually know when we are going into tough situations, but we spend most of our time worrying about the emotions of the situation rather than stepping back and coming up with a strategy that will pull the plug and take the charge out of it.

The other thing to remember is that we have more power than we sometimes realize. When we encounter the grumbling and mumbling of our detractors, we don't have to listen. There are plenty of people—some who are bullies, others who are just determined—who know they only have to say something loud and forceful to get people to back off. If you want proof of that, just watch some of those cable news talk shows.

I wonder how many of you are reading this book at a moment when your biggest detractor is your boss. I got a good laugh out of something Alex Sink told me. "Sometimes you are going to wind up working for a bad boss," she said. "Assess the situation. Figure out how bad it is, how long it is going to last, and if you can figure out a way to get along with the bad boss in order to get what you really want."

It's easy to slide into negativity and bolt too soon just to end an unpleasant moment. That may eliminate the pain, but cut you out of the reward you have worked hard to get. "A lot of people will go to work for a bad boss and say, 'That's it. I'm out of here.' But, sometimes, you have to lose some battles in order to win the war," Sink said. "I had a few bad bosses. Sometimes, I figured how to get out of their departments. The way to do that was to make them look good, to do a really good job; convince them they would look better to promote me out of their departments."

Why would they promote her if they knew she didn't like him? Sink just laughed. Her bad bosses had no clue she was unhappy. "I'm a Southern girl and I was taught to smile and like everybody," she said sheepishly. "Don't get mad. Get even." Sometimes you fight, sometimes you smile. But, you march through the tough spots.

Tune Out the Naysayers

Naysayers are the pessimists who tell you that you can't, you shouldn't, or you'll never. They're always around to stomp over your dreams, scare you out of taking chances, or make you feel like you just don't have what it takes. Pam Iorio knows all about naysayers. She is the popular Tampa politician who dropped an unexpected, late bomb on the political poobahs who'd just about anointed someone else their next mayor. The people loved her, but the power brokers weren't about to welcome her coming in so late.

"There was a period of time when all I got was negative," she remembered. One of the candidates had $600,000 in the bank and was on his way to raising a million dollars. She was told, "He has an army of people the likes of which have never been seen before on the political stage. There is going to be a walking campaign with 1,000 volunteers sweeping the neighborhoods." Other people told her she wouldn't be able to raise more than $50,000 because all of the money was tied up for the other candidates. "What those folks didn't know is that when people talk to me like that, it really gets me going. I thought, *Well, nobody thinks I can do it. That's interesting. I think I'll take that challenge.*"

Sometimes, the best way to neutralize a detractor is to put on your blinders and just charge ahead. On January 6, Iorio announced she would run. The election was March 4, and she figured if she could just make it to a runoff, she'd have a chance. She rallied people, not players, and that was easy because the people knew her and loved her. Her army was made up of family, friends, loyal poll workers, and average citizens.

Chalk one up for the underdog. In the first round, Iorio took 46 percent of the vote. She swept to victory in the runoff with 64 percent of the vote, even though her opponent raised twice as much money as she. "Make sure you don't live your life listening to naysayers," Iorio explained. "Don't let them control your destiny or your future. They don't control it. You control your future. You should take advice and you should take in information and you ought to be analytical so you aren't going after some pie-in-the-sky goal that is not attainable. But, if you believe something is attainable, then don't listen to the naysayers. You won't get anywhere if you do."

Sometimes going into battle is simply a matter of maintaining resolve when others want you to give up. Just ask Ann Rubenstein Tisch, whose vision of an all-girls' school in Harlem *really* annoyed the status quo. Perseverance is power, and Tisch hated being told she couldn't do what she wanted to do. "When I know it is the right thing, I have always tried to trust my instincts. People may say, 'You can't do that.' Well, why?" Tisch recalled lessons learned during her heroic battle to build the Young Women's Leadership School in East Harlem. "Why shouldn't those kids in Harlem have the same chance?" she asked. There were many people who didn't share her vision, but she learned to stay on track.

"You have to just blow off the naysayers who insist that what you are doing is impossible," she said. "Have ten minutes of angst about it, go home, call them every name in the book, complain to your nearest and dearest about how stupid everyone is, get it out of your system, then go on. There is absolutely no value added to stewing over the negative things people say to you. That, I've learned." Publicly, the criticism was flying in reaction to her plan to create a public all-girls' school. The American Civil Liberties Union, the National Organization for Women, New York Civil Rights Coalition all insisted the school was discriminatory, but Tisch believed that an all-girls' school would give its students the attention the girls needed to transcend the limits so many faced at home. The battle over the school was on the front page of the *New York Times* and was featured on *60 Minutes*. "It was so intense that, at one point during the coverage, a close relative said, 'You have got to get out of this.' My husband and I looked at him and said, 'Get out of this?

What? We aren't getting out of this because it is a little hot out there now.' He said, 'They are going to make mincemeat out of you.' We said, 'So be it. We aren't going away.' " Tisch's determination was fueled by her "sidewalk surveys," where she would ask people on the streets or in the subways if they would want such a school for their child. So many of those parents were exasperated with the public school system. All they wanted was something that would work. Now the school is one of the best attended in the city. Its standardized test scores are second only to Stuyvesant High School, one of the finest in the country. "Even our critics have come to write about this and say, 'I still don't like the idea of the school, but I can't argue that it's not doing what it set out to do.' "

So, do your own sidewalk surveys. Check in with your loved ones and with strangers. But don't give skeptics the power to kill your dream with their negativity. Just know what you want to do and why you want to do it. Then, *go do it.*

When you stand out front, you're going to take a few shots. Your mother may have said to consider the source, but sometimes the source is a friend or someone we respect. Then what? Or, what happens when we take our shot publicly, and the criticism is unjust?

It sure doesn't feel good. "People are going to impugn your motives for a lot of reasons," said Christine Todd Whitman, the former New Jersey governor and former chief of the Environmental Protection Agency. "The most important thing to remember is to always make an effort to reach out to people and explain why it is you are doing what you are doing, rather than just closing down and feeling they are all after you because you are a woman or this is a dog-eat-dog world. That's the biggest mistake."

Famed playwright Eve Ensler, who wrote *The Vagina Monologues,* withstood an attack by a good friend who wasn't included in the celebrated V-day performance in Madison Square Garden, which featured everyone from Oprah to Lilly Tomlin and Jane Fonda. A day later, this friend ran a raving attack of Ensler on her website. "It broke my heart," Ensler said. "For a week, even though Madison Square Garden had been so great, it left me destroyed. Every time I survive something like that, I get clear about who I am. I bless everyone who has attacked or criticized me for making me stronger."

Since the publication and staging of *The Vagina Monologues,* there have been female critics who have attacked Ensler's work. That shocks her. "I think a lot of the reason women attack other women has to do with jealousy. Look, we've been trained to be jealous. We've been programmed to be jealous. If you have jealousy, go do the opposite of what your feelings are telling you so you can correct it in yourself. Women won't get ahead unless they support each other. When women support each other, they flourish. They thrive. When women don't, it's deadly."

Ensler reiterated what I have heard hundreds of other women say: it hurts extra when the negativity comes from another woman—one of us—because we want that support. "You expect men not to support you," Ensler said. "They are in another world, function in another zone. Women know how hard it is for themselves and other women to get ahead in this world. When one puts you down, you think, *Is she forgetting what it's like in here?*"

I wondered if Ensler confronted the friend who'd posted the criticism. You know how a lot of us are. We'd rather grumble over it than clash. But, Ensler said, "I wrote her a letter and said I was heartbroken. She tried to minimize what she'd written, but left it on her website. It still hurts me."

Ensler's honesty is refreshing, and so on the mark. Part of the reason we don't like what naysayers say is because dissent hurts, especially when it comes from someone we love or trust. It feeds into our own insecurities that we somehow don't measure up. You can bask in the applause from thousands of people, as Ensler did in Madison Square Garden, then fixate on the one blast of negativity that somehow reinforces your own worries that you are not worthy or loved. Or, you could look at it and see how mean you are being to yourself. Imagine what we could accomplish if we would all just lighten up on ourselves.

A MOMENT OF
DEFIANCE
WITH
Erin Brockovich

Everybody calls her "the real Erin Brockovich." Julia Roberts's Academy Award–winning performance in the film Erin Brockovich *turned the real Brockovich's life story into a mustang legend. Working as a file clerk at the firm of Masry & Vititoe, Brockovich stumbled across records that led her to unravel the frightening aftereffects of continued exposure to toxic Chromium 6 in the community of Hinkley, California. Brockovich proved that the Pacific Gas and Electric Company's compressor station had leaked the Chromium 6 into the groundwater, unleashing a health nightmare for residents. When she and Masry were done, PG&E paid a $333 million settlement to Hinkley's 600 residents. It was the largest lawsuit of its kind, and Masry surprised Brockovich with a $2 million bonus. She continues to work at the firm as director of research in high-profile cases.*

I have nothing to gain or lose. Fire me from my job, put me down, do what you want to me. It's not going to change anything, because if you do or do not like me, fine. I don't frankly care.

I was born and raised in Kansas and never thought of myself as an attractive woman. I was geeky, freckly, lanky, and I had crooked teeth and a learning disability. I'm dyslexic. My disability is what opened the door for me to be a more forgiving person, more open to other ideas and issues and thoughts. I didn't have the book smarts to be someone who would graduate from college and make money and be something. I never felt attractive and I never felt intelligent. I've read a bazillion self-help books because I never felt worthy. I had zero dollars in the bank and I didn't have self-esteem. When I had a $2 million bonus in the bank, I still didn't have it. We think we'll get it once we get a nice house, a nice car, breast implants, and a chance to keep up with the Joneses. We always think the grass is greener, but it's not.

After I got that bonus, I was physically ill because of all that time I spent in Hinkley. I couldn't get out of bed to enjoy it. I had money, but I had been an absent mom to my children and I tried to make it up to them by giving them two TVs in their room and puppies and all of that. I had two children with drug addictions. I spent $250,000 getting them in the right schools and rehab programs. You've got money? So what? Your true character exists regardless, and you have to get in touch with it.

My self-esteem is so much greater than it was in the past, but not because of the bonus or the movie. It was because of the Hinkley experience that made me appreciate the environment and the gift of health. What made me feel good about myself was being able to be helpful to another person through my work. That made me a better person. You can have all the money you want, but what is truly the mark you leave? It's the sense of doing something outside of yourself—as a senseless act. I didn't do Hinkley because I thought there was going to be money. I had no idea that Ed was going to give me a bonus or that there was going to be a movie about it. I did it because I wanted to help people. I did it because that's how I was raised. I was curious, I wanted to help, and I applied common sense. I put all those things into play. People saw a movie. They saw Julia Roberts. The process wasn't about me or the movie. It was a bigger cause. All I did was uncover PG&E's lie.

I don't know what people do or don't get about me. I have a real strong sense of myself. I know what my priorities are. They are ingrained in me. I believe we all have the right to know the truth. I am so tired of the ignorance in people who want to bury their heads in the sand. You know, "Why should I worry? It's not my kid." You should worry because someday it's going to be you or your child. We are entitled to protect our families and our health because those are the most valuable, precious gifts we have. I don't know why people don't always get that. You don't realize the gift of your health until you lose it. It is something we take for granted.

Simple decisions you make will affect other people. Make decisions with that in mind, respecting other people and human health and life. Some things don't have to be logical. Listen to your heart and gut.

Get in touch with the pure simplicity that exists in every single day that we take for granted. First and foremost, remember your health. And those clichés we grew up with like, "Take time to stop and smell the roses," or "Feel the warmth of the sun on your face." We take these things for granted until we are sick or dying and can't get them back. Wouldn't it be nice to appreciate them when the world is at its best or when you feel your best? Do you ever wonder where we go when we die? I don't know, but I know I can't take the house, I can't take the (fake) boobs, and my looks won't matter. I can only hope I left something behind about believing in yourself and taking care of your children.

Honesty is all you've got. Everything that bothers me in life is dishonesty. You can call me a do-gooder, but at the end of the day, I can live with myself. How about you?

7.

VERBAL COMBAT

Saying What You Mean

THERE'S an old saying, "Never get in a pissing match with a skunk." Well, there sure are a lot of skunks out there, and sometimes you don't have a choice. How do you win when you're being sprayed? With information, facts, and the confidence that you know what you are talking about. It takes a lot of courage to speak up. Sometimes, we wait way too long, until we are raw with anger.

One woman who has taught me how to keep my foot on the floor, rather than in my mouth is Sam Horn, the author of five books, including *Tongue Fu*™ and *What's Holding You Back?* She is best known as the "master of martial arts for the mind and mouth." So how do we prepare so we are not tongue-tied when something unfair, unkind, or inappropriate happens? I'm sick of coming up with the perfect retort once I'm heading home in my car.

Here's Horn's theory: First, when you don't know what to say, don't say anything. Especially, don't say the "I" word. For example, if someone says, "You are so emotional and defensive," and you say, "I am not emotional and defensive," well, suddenly you are. "You can see any denial debate of an accusation will create an argument where we are going back and forth—yes you are, no I'm not, yes you are, no I'm not," Horn explained. Instead of engaging, reverse the dynamic, asking, "What do you mean?" or, "What makes you say that?" or, "Why do you think that?" Horn said that puts the conversational ball back in their court. If their concerns are legitimate, those questions and subsequent answers will reveal the real issue. You can deal with the issue, instead of the attack. If they are just taunting you, the questions force them to explain themselves.

"One of the most important things for women to understand in the business world is that verbal sparring is normal. This is how men relate. They taunt and ridicule each other. They ridicule each other, and it really is a pecking order kind of thing," Horn said. If you come back and say, "Do other people fall for this?" or, "Do other people let you talk to them like this?" it neutralizes the tension. Ronald Reagan was the master of this. During his campaign for president, rival Jimmy Carter took a shot

The Rules of Verbal Engagement

1. Your goal is not to win. It is to create a winning climate.
2. Win-win is always better than win-lose.
3. Consider the end result you are after. What is the easiest way to get that result?
4. A short-term victory will generally rear up and bite you somewhere down the line.
5. Maybe men can get away with cursing or talking harshly, but women have to do it with great caution.
6. If you're going to cry, try to do it out of the sight of your detractors.
7. If you are convinced you've got to vent, do it verbally. Put things in writing only when you need a written record and only when you have calmed down.
8. Don't feel bad if you have blundered in verbal combat. We all have. Mustangs instinctively know how to run. Sometimes we need help with the walk.

at him for being against national health insurance. Reagan fired back, "There you go again." There was absolutely no content in that comeback. His delivery was humorous, quick, and biting. He blew Carter away, and the moment was seen as a turning point in his campaign.

We need to know how to protect ourselves with our words and our paperwork. Take notes in meetings, then write casual e-mails or memos reminding your boss "So glad you liked my suggestion that x, y, and z . . ." That way you don't have to pound your fist on the table, shouting, "That was my idea!" It's all recorded and documented in a very subtle way.

Consider the Timing

As you debate whether to go into battle, consider the timing. Horn has a friend who'd been given several months off because she had a very difficult pregnancy and birth. Within a month of coming back, she found out her salary was substantially less than what other department heads were making. Understandably, the woman was furious, and told Horn that as soon as she went back to work, she was going to march in and demand the inequity be rectified. Obviously, the woman was right. Still, Horn cautioned her. "I said, 'Debbie, is it good timing? It doesn't matter if it is unfair. It's hard, after being off for so many months, for you to march in and make a demand after they were so kind.' I told her to wait a couple of months, then go in and see if she could get it rectified. The point is not whether you are right or wrong. The point is, are they in a receptive mood?" Her friend waited a few months, then went in and got the problem fixed.

What should we do when we're in a meeting, and we put an idea out there and it is ignored, then ten minutes later some guy voices the same idea, and suddenly the men in the room think it is the most brilliant thing they have ever heard in their lives? "Well, if it's innocent, or it's the first time he's done it, it's small stuff," Horn said. "But, if it is intentional and persistent, and say your idea is going to be a big revenue-producing project, it's not only smart for you to speak up, but it is absolutely necessary." She'd use his name and actually interrupt the conversation by saying, "Joe, before we go any further, let's clarify something. I'm glad you are excited about this. When I brought this up about ten minutes ago, it's exactly what I meant. I'm glad you like it, too. It looks like you have some good suggestions on how we can carry this out." Do it before he gets any steam with the idea. It's a subtle and assertive way to reclaim your idea, Horn said. Plus, you aren't accusing the idea thief of anything.

Do Your Homework

Don't fight with emotion. Fight with information. Almost every successful woman who I have asked about dealing with detractors, hecklers, enemies, and critics has told me that information is, perhaps, the most mighty weapon that we've all got at our disposal. "Whatever you do, don't lose your head," said television anchorwoman and former prosecutor Nancy Grace. "Strategize your argument. When you engage, engage with information. Don't let emotions clog your logic. When I'd prepare my case, I'd immediately prepare for their case, so I knew what to expect."

If you are going into battle, prepare for battle. The only way to do that is with facts and effort. "Work like hell," Grace said. "Enjoy the knowledge. I recall sitting in the law library on Saturday, Sunday, and holidays. I'd look out the window and see people having a wonderful weekend, but in my mind's eye, I would imagine the defense attorney playing golf or going to the movie or having a beer. I would just lick my chops. I knew they were out somewhere with no idea that I was working on it. It takes an incredible amount of time and thinking and planning and plotting, but it is worth it."

Grace said she never lets the other side know when it has landed a blow. "I would keep a stone face when it happened. I learned that in court. Why would I want a jury to know that I just got a kick in the pants? It would make their victory sweeter if they knew. Plus, you keep the other side at a disadvantage when they are not quite sure they've won on something."

Interior Secretary Gale Norton stays her course and deals with detractors by being analytical and steadfast, spending time figuring out what position is right for her. Once she's convinced she's right, she stands firm. "It comes from doing all my homework and making sure I've really convinced myself of a position. The people on the other side frequently haven't thought it through as strongly as I have," she said. "When I am under attack in a situation where I feel I have done the right thing and I have taken the right position, it doesn't bother me. I probably should be more bothered by it, but I really feel the confidence from knowing we've done the best we can. We've done our homework."

There are hundreds of questions you can ask yourself, and remember, making sure you have the information you need doesn't mean you have permission to stall taking action until you have unearthed every single detail. There are *always* more details. Just know your facts. Be ready for everything. You don't have to bore people with your homework, either. Information is the ammo in your arsenal.

Watch for Red Flags

Why do people lie, manipulate, undermine, and stab others in the back? Because they can. If you think it's time for a moment of truth and to confront someone, be realistic. Do you really expect a backstabber to suddenly develop a conscience and tell you everything? When someone is trying to do something underhanded, it is unlikely he or she is going to stop everything and confess the minute you become suspicious—at least, not without a little help. Let me dig into my arsenal of tools from my years as an investigative reporter and tell you a little about being effective in the middle of confrontation.

First, people often lie through omission and/or embellishment. Think of how many times you've asked someone a question only to get an answer to exactly what you've asked, and nothing more. The person knows full well what you are after, but he or she doesn't have to volunteer anything. Remember Bill Clinton in his grand jury testimony? If the President of the United States can hide the truth by arguing the meaning of the word "is," then imagine what the people around you can do. Teenagers will do it every time. "Did you sneak out in the car after we went to bed?" you might ask. You'll get a straight answer of "no," because the kid had the nerve to steal off with your car while you were still awake!

Watch out for certain red-flag words and phrases that will alert you to a liar almost every time. When you start hearing someone say, "Trust me," "To be 100 percent honest," "Believe me," and "Honestly," listen very, very closely. Red flags! If you hear things like, "Not that I can remember," "To the best of my knowledge," "Why would I," "Do you think I'm so stupid that I would," pay especially close attention. All of those phrases are designed to throw you off, but when you get the drill, you can be even more effective. If a question is answered with another question, take note because the person may be deciding whether to lie or tell the truth, or debating how big of a lie to tell. When those tricks don't work, he or she might try a memory lapse, and try to throw you off with a simple, "Not that I can think of" or, "To the best of my knowledge." What do you do when that happens? Try saying, "Well, I think you need to try a little harder," or, "That technique doesn't work with me."

In your conversation, you may see tactics people use to minimize what happened. For example, someone who has embezzled money might say he just "borrowed" it. A husband who has cheated by doing everything but intercourse may be able to convince you that it isn't nearly what you think. Companies are masters of saying they are "expanding" or "repackaging" when they are really cutting services. Liars often have a story ready, just in case. And if it sounds rehearsed, it probably is. Or, he or she may concoct something in the moment. Let's say an employee is being wooed by an arch competitor who could gain valuable information by hiring her away. You ask if she's interviewed over there. "What?" she says. That buys her a little time. Or, "I couldn't hear you." Then, she might say, "Why would I do that?" or, "Do you think I would do that?" Stalling. You'll get the same thing from teenagers.

Physical cues are important, but only when they are used in combination. Just because someone's eye contact is lousy, it doesn't mean they are guilty. But, if you ask a tough question and he or she loses the eye contact, crosses the arms, and takes a defensive-looking posture, something might be going on. If you are trying to use this as a measure of whether or not they are telling the truth, just be alert to what changes, in what combination, and when the changes happen.

Finally, listen to your gut. You should not have to convince yourself to believe something that just doesn't seem right. Someone protesting too much is sending up red flags. If it seems all too urgent that you believe or disbelieve something, start to question why.

When *Not* to Engage

Let's take a minute to consider your option of staying out of the battle and doing nothing. That might be the best approach if the stakes are small or you aren't invested in the issue, and we mustangs have always got to be sure we aren't making more trouble for ourselves by fighting on every issue, especially when it comes to a personal attack. When something significant has happened and you remain silent, know what you are doing. Silence suggests the bad behavior is okay. Constant confrontation suggests you are a little crazed. I once had a co-worker really stick it to me by blabbing things I'd told her in confidence. She told everybody—my employees, my peers, even my bosses. I never once confronted her on what she'd done and, for almost two years, I tried to avoid her. I'd seethe whenever she'd walk by, but I never said a word because I knew whatever I said would have been blabbed, too.

What I didn't understand then, which I sure get now, is that we shouldn't avoid confrontation because we are afraid it will lead to others talking about us behind our backs. If it's gotten this far, they're probably *already* talking behind our backs. I now have a method of confronting backstabbers that says I don't condone the bad behavior, makes it clear I want it stopped, and doesn't give the person much grist for gossip. What I say is this: "I know what you did/said, and I want you to stop." The person then acts all shocked and begs, "What? What did I do/say?" To which I say, "I'm not going to engage with you on this, but you know." Then, I walk away as they are still saying, "Wait! I don't know! What do you think I did?" It's just beautiful.

The "I'm not going to engage" tactic works with emotional situations *and* intellectual arguments. I've heard many people lament that they aren't verbally quick enough to win an argument. I know what they mean. If I can think for a bit and write everything down, I can generally out-argue anybody. But, on the spot? Forget it. Well, there are certainly times when all you need to say is, "Look, I'm not going to engage with you on this." They'll try again, and you just repeat, "I'm not going to get into this with you." Then, walk away. I used to work with an arrogant, opinionated guy who could verbally out-argue me on anything, in part because he knew his facts and in part because he always got very loud and seemed so certain. I couldn't stand talking to him. Finally, I said, "Sorry, George, I'm not going to engage with you on this." I think he took it as a sign that I didn't consider him worthy of my attention, which was okay with me. It made him crazy. "Why not!" he said, as he leapt out from behind his desk. "George, I'm not going to engage with you on this." I used to routinely lose arguments with the guy. After that, I never lost another. At first, I'd just repeat my line. After a couple of weeks, he knew not to even try.

When All Else Fails in Verbal Combat

Rely on old high school debate tricks:

When you want to gain ground incrementally, you can say, "Don't you agree that . . ."

If the other person makes a good point that you don't wish to address, just say, "*That's* not the point *This* is the point," and reframe the discussion to what you want to talk about.

Watch talk TV on cable some night. Those blowhards do that all the time. Don't let anyone tell *you* what the point is. But, you can sure try to tell *them!*

Finally, there is another theory that, if you repeat yourself enough times with great conviction, you'll win your argument. The more you repeat it, the more they will get it. Just say the same thing over and over again. When you encounter opposition, just start with a "Yes, but . . ." and repeat yourself one more time.

Okay, consider yourself briefed. Know that:

1. You'll find yourself in a few intense situations.

2. You'll get through them.

It takes a long time to feel comfortable in this part of the mustang arena, but be tough, be clever, and don't let your emotions push you off the cliff.

A MOMENT OF
MISSION
WITH
Nancy Grace

Nancy Grace planned to be married to the love of her life and go into teaching. At age 21, her fiancé was murdered, forever changing her mission and drive. Now the former prosecutor is a regular fixture on Court TV and CNN, Grace has become a fierce advocate of victim rights.

As a prosecutor, I never told anyone about losing Keith. I feared some defense attorney could somehow bring his murder out to a jury and suggest there was some sort of vendetta. I didn't want to jeopardize any of my cases. Even, to this day, it is difficult to talk about it. It is always like cold water in the face, and it is still very, very upsetting.

It felt as if my whole world had exploded. Like I'd been on a beautiful, hand-painted merry-go-round that suddenly stopped. It's surprising that the world kept turning. Up until then, I had no knowledge of evil or violence. It not only robbed me of my dreams for my whole life, but of the whole world.

I really want other victims to know that they are not alone. I hate that word people use: "closure." It's like, if you break your arm and don't get it fixed, but you learn to flip pancakes anyway. I've never been the same person I was before Keith's murder. Yet, I am very blessed.

I don't feel powerful. It's important that I try to keep that violence from happening to other people. I feel like I am a piece of driftwood at sea, fighting against some huge world. If I were powerful, none of this would have happened. Victims have no power in our system. I feel invincible. I feel I am doing something right. I didn't live through all those years of pain for anybody—any defense attorney or judge—to stop me now.

It's hard to tell someone else what that feeling is like, that feeling you can't rest until you try to set something right. I probably would have had the family and home I'd dreamed of, if I had not believed I had been called to do something about it. I felt unhappy with the system. Fine. Change it, even if it means you become a part of it. I just couldn't take it lying down.

I was very poor growing up in rural Georgia. If I can graduate from NYU and land at Court TV and CNN, let me tell you, anybody can do it! If I could win a hundred jury trials, you can win a hundred jury trials. I am nobody from nowhere, and I'm proud of it. It means anybody can do it if you want to work, if you want to work triple time. There were many, many nights when I would leave the courtroom or the law library exhausted. I could hardly haul my cartons of research behind me. I would think of Keith and would gain strength, believing that, somehow, I was making good out of bad.

If you are going to jump, jump. Don't second-guess. If you want anybody else to believe in you, you have got to believe in what you are saying. If you screw up, pause and explain. You'll get a chance.

I'm told I'm 5'1", but I think I'm 6'3". Nobody ever told me I couldn't. I don't think I am anything special, but I think my message is special. It's more important than me or anything I could ever dream of. I had a lot of labels attached to me when I started doing TV: "Ellie May (from the *Beverly Hillbillies*) with a law degree," or "The dumb blond with the Southern accent." I really do believe, if you dwell on labels, you are wasting a lot of energy that you could be using to do a much better job. Think of the energy you waste when you worry about what somebody else thinks of you. Does it matter? If I really am Ellie May with a law degree, who cares? So, fine.

If you don't want to get dirty, stay out of the mud fight. When your beliefs require you to stand up and fight, then fight rather than die watching.

When roll is called, I want to say I tried.

8

THE BIG ASK

Getting What You Want

WHEN my first book came out, everyone I knew was telling me the same thing. It was not "Congratulations" or "Good job!" Oh no. They all said, "Gee, you really need to get your book on *Oprah*." Like all I needed to do was snap my fingers and Oprah Winfrey would personally come to Tampa, begging me to let her turn my book into an international bestseller. I heard it again and again and again, whether I was in my home state of Florida or visiting Switzerland. I heard it from complete strangers and best friends, not to mention my mother. Everybody—I mean *everybody*—says it. Oprah, Oprah, Oprah, Oprah.

One day, my neighbor Dave called to me from across the street. "You ought to get your book on *Oprah*!" he shouted.

"I know, Dave," I said in frustration. "I know. So, do you know any of the producers?"

He shrugged, and said quite matter of factly, "Why don't you just get Cokie Roberts to call her?"

Yeah, right. "I barely know Cokie Roberts," I replied. "I interviewed her for an hour on the telephone. She doesn't know me."

"Well," he said, no hesitation, "she's on the cover of your book. Just call her up and ask."

"I can't do that," I said.

"Why not?" he asked, incredulous.

It has since struck me, what if I *had* asked? One of two things would have happened. Roberts would have said yes, or Roberts would have said no. If she'd said no, I'm sure she wouldn't have spent much more than a few moments thinking about me, the presumptuous author who dared to bother her by asking for a favor. Maybe she'd have said no because it would have bothered *her* to ask Oprah's people for a favor. Regardless, Roberts is a good woman who does care about mentoring and connecting with other women. When I interviewed her, she told me how much joy she experienced when younger women would come to her and ask advice in terms of work or family. "A lot of it is like the old conversations that happened over the backyard fence, where women of different generations would visit," Roberts said. "A lot of that takes place in the workplace now, and it's a nice thing. 'Do you think my baby's ready for solid food and how do I deal with this supervisor who is giving me trouble?' I think it is so important to seek wisdom at whatever you are doing." Looking at that, I'll bet that if Roberts hadn't been willing to make the call, she'd have given me a few names and ideas.

I had nothing to lose by asking, but I never did make that call.

Two years later, Roberts and I were speaking for the same group, and I told her about my neighbor suggesting I get her to call Oprah Winfrey on my behalf.

"Just out of curiosity," I said, "what would you have done if I had called and asked for the favor?"

"Couldn't have done it for you," she laughed. "I've never been able to get *my* books on *Oprah*!"

What strikes me about my neighbor's suggestion is this: he didn't think it was any big deal to ask for a favor. A lot of men don't. Granted, many of these guys will drive around lost for hours because they don't want to ask for directions, but they aren't afraid to ask for professional assistance because they know how the game is played. Men ask for favors all the time, perhaps because they think they deserve the help. They return favors, too. They play the "I'll scratch your back if you scratch mine" game while we hold ourselves back, too timid to ask for anything. We miss opportunities because we are socialized to do for others and put ourselves last. Even though so many women have committed to mentoring us toward success, we are still afraid of what I call "The Big Ask."

Don't Ask, Don't Get

Even when someone hands us a phone number or offers to make the connection for us, many of us are too chicken to take advantage of the opportunity. I know a young woman who wants to find work on the business end of the recording industry. A colleague of her mother's passed a phone number to her, the direct line to his daughter, one of the top executives at one of America's largest labels. He even told his daughter to expect the call, but the call never came. The young woman who had been handed the phone number, introduction, and opportunity was too afraid to follow through. That is not an unusual story. We constantly let opportunity slip away from us because we don't follow through properly.

"Don't ask? Don't get," said AT&T president Betsy Bernard. "What's the worst thing somebody could say? The one thing you know for sure is if you don't ask, you're not going to get it for sure."

You can't move ahead without a few favors, said playwright Eve Ensler. "If you ask people for something, it often makes them happy to do things, and then they are allowed to ask for something in return. One of the great things about being successful is that you can do something for someone else."

People in power will help you, but you just have to ask for their help. I asked the retired banking trailblazer Alex Sink what she would have done if a teller wrote her a letter asking for a little mentoring and career advice. "I'd have taken him or her to lunch," Sink said. "Always ask for help. Always. Get a lot of different opinions because people have different points of view about things."

Comedian and actress Sandra Bernhard said she is uncomfortable asking for help, but "you have to get past that voice that says you shouldn't ask for things, because asking is taking advantage of people.

People ask me, and I'm glad to give them help, usually." If a young performer wants help and has talent, she might give the person a job, an invite to tour on the road, or a chance to open for her. "At least I can put a little money in their pocket. It's something I like to do."

Are you hearing this? *Ask*. There is nothing to lose. Do you realize what you will gain by giving up on that fear of asking for favors or help? I am constantly asking others to invest in me, whether it is by giving me an interview for a book or hiring me to speak for an event. I learned how to make my way in the speaking business because I asked successful speakers to mentor me on how *they* did it. Not only did they teach me, but their help accelerated my career to the point where I was able to make my living as a speaker within a year of starting my business. If I'd done it the slow way—feeling my way through the dark, trying to guess what I should do, and hoping for the best—I would likely have given up after a few months, discouraged and broke. If the information is out there, and other people have it, *go get it*.

Successful people will help you. They want to help you. All you have to do is recruit them to your cause. I have sent countless letters and e-mails to successful people asking if I could just connect with them for an hour of mentoring. Usually, I end the letter by promising to mentor someone else in exchange for their help. I have been turned down once, by a woman who was so unfriendly that I realized going to lunch with her would have been a waste of *my* time. My lunch money was much better spent on the dozens of others who have come through when I asked for their help.

When it came to getting my book on *Oprah,* the advice of one marketing person actually helped me to succeed. I'd written Oprah's people 29 letters and personally delivered books to the Harpo studios. She told me how to focus my letters better. After that, the book made the show, and my mentors cheered.

Ask. Ask. Ask. Ask. Ask. Ask. Ask. Ask.

360-Degree Networking

Many people don't know who to ask for help. My guide to networking goes like this: network up, down, and sideways. Your best asset is not your resume, your credentials, or your list of accomplishments. It is *you*. You are bold enough to build a network, and you are worthy enough to turn professional contacts into friends who will help you achieve your goals.

NETWORK UP

This means finding one mentor—or several—with the knowledge, power, or clout to help you get the information, education, and connections you need to propel you forward toward your goal. Let's say you want to move up in your company. Identify someone in power who knows what you need to know. Make contact and say, "I'm trying to learn more about x, y, and z. You know plenty about those things, and I wondered whether we might get together for coffee." Or lunch. Or a brief meeting. I don't recommend asking for drinks or dinner. There is something about requesting evening time that suggests a boundary violation.

You can network up outside your organization, as well. If you are starting your own business, be smart about who you ask for advice. Let's say you are going to open a coffee shop. Don't get the competitor down the street to mentor you, because he or she has a vested interest in seeing you fail. Call someone across town, or even in another city. In a corporate environment, you can even write the CEO of your company and, perhaps, get a meeting. You might get blown off, but, the mere fact that you have asked for help suggests that you care about your career within the company. Anyone who laughs at or minimizes your efforts is somebody who has his or her own issues.

Finally, be mindful of the climate of your company and make sure you don't violate the rules of the chain of command. If there is an open-door policy, you shouldn't have to worry about it. But, it is often a good idea to cover yourself by letting your direct supervisor know you are making an informal contact with a superior. That can be threatening to some bosses, so you can minimize the concern by saying, "I'm doing a speech for my alumni group [or whatever] and wrote a note to John to see if he had a few minutes to give me some input. I'd like your input, as well." There may be someone in an influential position in another company who can give you another perspective. Avoid contacting a direct competitor to your current employer unless you are in the market for another job. But there is no harm done if you are in human resources in a telecommunications company and you ask for help from someone in human resources at a bank.

"You can't get anything done without people helping you, and the only way they can help you is if you ask for it," said former Texas governor Ann Richards. "My experience has been that when you ask for help, people are so pleased and so flattered that someone cares about their opinion and stature that they are thrilled to give it. You may not even know what it is specifically that you want to ask for. You may simply want to get to know someone better who has stature and has the ability to help you get things done. What women have not learned is that the worst thing that can happen to them is the other person can say no. In that case, you just go to the next person on the list and ask them." Richards entertains many such requests. "All they have to do is ask me," she said. "The first thing they should do is ask for an appointment. They should set a specific amount of time they want to spend with me on the first go-around. Not more than 30 minutes. They should say, 'Here, in general, is what I want to talk to you about.' I should know all of that before they walk in." That's where the discussion starts. Where it often leads is to "The Big Ask." Will Richards make a call or two to help? If so, "I'll pick up the phone while we are sitting there. I'll make the call right there, rather than putting it off. If I get busy, I may forget."

> "The worst thing that can happen to you is that the person can say no. In that case, you just go to the next person on the list and ask them."
>
> —ANN RICHARDS

NETWORK SIDEWAYS

This is where many would-be success stories get trapped in the box. There are dozens of organizations that attract new executives or business owners. They make a big deal out of introducing everybody, networking and swapping business cards. These are great places to go for commiserating, but they are terrible places to network toward your success because most of the people you are networking with are struggling to succeed, just like you. It's like doing business in the sandbox. "I'll do business with you if you'll do business with me" is not enough to propel you to certain success. Those people don't know what you need to know and generally don't have the contacts to get you where you want to go.

But, what they do offer is not only important, but sometimes life saving. They are in the trenches fighting, too. They know what you are going through. Plus, you don't know which of your peers is going to make it big and be able to help you later. Do *not* ignore these networking opportunities! Your sideways network will pick you up when you feel beaten by obstacles. These friends will get you ready to get back in the game, and provide some of the most important emotional support you will find. In addition, your sideways network has its own professional network of people who really are in a position to help you.

Share what you know and who you know with your sideways network, and in return, that network will share with you. These people are great for telling you what they have tried that has not worked, or how they have overcome a set of obstacles. They will be your best friends as you face your obstacles, and even though these contacts can't put your success on the fast track, they can stand behind you cheering.

NETWORK DOWN

This is the most important approach, and it is something I will tell you over and over and over again. You want mentoring? Be a mentor. You want help? Give help. If you want the ability to ask "The Big Ask," you've got to be willing to offer up "The Big Answer" whenever you can. Take the freedom to ask for favors, but entertain the same kinds of requests from people who want the knowledge, access, and insight *you* have already gained. Perhaps you think you are so low on the totem pole that you have nothing to offer, but you are wrong. The fact that you are even in the hierarchy means you likely know how someone on the outside can get in the door. Help others. That's the way it works.

The Anatomy of "The Big Ask"

There is a subtle art to asking for help. You don't want to sound too desperate or arrogant. You sure don't want to sound like a user. I used to teach college journalism courses, and one of my students bought me a beautiful gift just before I got married. I was touched, and I told her how much I appreciated her kindness. "Knowing you is going to be very good for my career," she said in response.

I realize there is a possibility I misinterpreted it, that she was actually complimenting my success, but I don't think so. I think she thought the tray would keep her in my favor so I would give her good references and contacts. I'll help just about anybody for free, but not someone who intends to buy me with a tray and four coasters. Use that lesson as a reminder of the subtle approach that will get you far more than saying,

Finding Your Mentors Through Power Networking

1. You've figured out which direction you would like to head with your career. Who are the key people within your company who are in positions to help you accomplish your goals? Who are people in similar positions at other companies who have the knowledge that could make you more savvy with your own career progression? Who are the three people among the ten you've just selected who you wish to initially target as mentors? Also, what do you hope to gain from each person?
2. Brainstorm your contact letter. Instead of sending a letter that says, "I am writing you to ask that you do x and y for me," come up with something that says, "I need a little mentoring. Because I am so impressed by what you've done, I'm hoping I might be able to talk you into lunch." Come up with your own approach that sounds like you.
3. Now, have a punchy, one-paragraph summary of who you are and what you are after. Don't list every company you have worked for or every kind of job you have ever had. Just give the high points.

"Hey, can I meet so you can give me a big promotion?" or, "Let's have lunch so you can introduce me to your friends and they can help me to make a lot of money." Much better to say, "I need a little mentoring," or, "Do you have any advice for tracking my career upward?"

The person you are professionally courting will know you are hoping for some benefit, otherwise you wouldn't be asking for help. But, don't be transparent about it. You don't have to appeal to that person's ego with effusive flattery. Merely showing a genuine respect for what that person has learned and accomplished is flattering enough.

The more you do this, the easier it gets, and the information and lessons you absorb will help you in other ways. U.S. Secretary of the Interior Gale Norton said she learned how to approach people when she was running for office as attorney general in Colorado. "Being a candidate is a great tool because you are forced to approach people you don't know," she said. "It's helpful for women to put themselves into situations where they have to project and show themselves, and to have practice in showing what they can do. I've always been an advocate that, if you're thinking about changing jobs, or changing careers, you should go out and talk to a lot of different people and explore a whole lot of different things. Partly, this is to find the place where you fit the best, but also, the practice of talking about yourself to other people is very helpful."

Letter writing is a great way to make the approach. Some people will start a letter saying, "So-and-so said I should write." Sometimes that works well. I prefer to start with an attention-getting line that piques the person's interest and wait to name-drop until the second or third sentence. Before you write your letter, you should have a good grasp on what you are asking for. There will be times when you are asking for brainpower—For example, "I was wondering if we might get together for 20 or 30 minutes so we can brainstorm ways to . . ." There will be times when you need connection—for example, "Is there any way we might get together for lunch? I need a little mentoring and know you have learned plenty about x, y, and z." You might even be asking for sponsorship or financial support—for example, "I know you are bombarded by fund-raisers, but your track record of helping people who [fill in the blank] tells me that, even if you don't contribute, you will know who will."

I've always thought it is better to shoot down their no argument up front. I've started letters, saying "I know. You're busy." Wanting mentoring on the bookselling business, I wrote the owner of The Tattered Cover, the nation's largest independent bookstore, "Since I spent half of my paycheck in your store during the eight years I lived in Denver, I figured you wouldn't mind giving me a little mentoring." The owner wouldn't give me a little mentoring, she gave me a *lot*. She gave me advice, names, and phone numbers. She hosted my favorite signing, and on the day of the big event, we had lunch. On a different occasion, I wrote to a major agent who was not taking new clients, saying, "Even though I am crushed that you won't represent me, could you spare time for a phone chat so I can find my way to the right person who will?" She did, and became a cheerleader for me as my book sold. Be creative, be fun, be sincere. When the risk is high that your letter will be ignored, take a chance. I figure it is better to risk making a bad impression than making no impression at all. I once sent cover letters looking for jobs that began, "Look, I know you're busy. I'll skip the bullshit." I heard back from every single person I wrote. I don't advise doing that in the corporate world. I was writing newspaper editors, who really love that word. But, it suggests you should know your audience!

Acknowledge that you are mindful and respectful of the person's busy schedule. Someone once called to ask me to spend an hour mentoring her daughter, who had just graduated college. I was completely on board until she said, "When shall I tell her you will give her an hour in the next week?" I was planning on giving the young woman a full afternoon in the next week, but resented being told that I *had* to do it and *when*. Just acknowledge in some way that you appreciate the favor. He or she does not have to do it on your timetable. Most of the people who are in positions to help have full agendas and no matter how much on the front burner your request is for you, it is likely a back-burner matter for the person you are contacting.

It doesn't matter what line of work you do. You'll always do better if you are able to get others to invest in you. If you are in sales, the challenge is to get somebody to buy something from you. If you are in management, the challenge is to get them to follow your lead. If you are in an entry level job, your advancement is dependent upon others thinking you are worth promoting. It's all about building solid networks. As a reporter, everything depends on your ability to get people to like and trust you. Novice reporters have to endure the drudgery of the ritual of "cop checks" several times a day. That means making calls to 30 or more law enforcement agencies to find out if any news is breaking. The temptation was always there to run through the list and say, "Hi, this is Fawn Germer from the *Miami Herald*. Anything going on? No? Okay, thanks. Click." But, I learned that if I cracked a few jokes with the person stuck answering the phone, they'd not only tell me what was up when I called, but *they* would call *me* so they could help me get the story first. That's what happens as you build your network up. You'll be calling so many assistants and secretaries and, hopefully, making alliances so you'll get their help because they like you and feel invested in your success. They'll nudge and remind the boss to get back to you. If you build a relationship with the gatekeeper to the boss, he or she will not mind being bugged by you.

There are times when persistence pays, and times when it doesn't. For my last book, I made about 80 calls to get an interview with Olympian Jackie Joyner-Kersee. Nothing worked. But, for this book, I spent a year writing letters to the people who could connect me with Susan Sarandon and AT&T President Betsy Bernard. Those letters, e-mails, and calls paid off. Chances are, if somebody has legions of assistants, an aide is going to read your letter. Just make sure you are approaching the right one. Aim as high as you reasonably can. You want to talk to a woman about succeeding in business? The odds of sitting down with Carly Fiorina, the CEO of Hewlett-Packard, aren't great. But, the odds of sitting down with somebody who is one or two steps away from her aren't bad.

Also, there is always more than one "right person" who can help you. Maybe you encounter a few negatives. No one person has the lock on the top. In my last book, I tried hard to get astronaut Sally Ride. Twice, she said no. Well, she's not the only astronaut in the world, and

Kathryn Sullivan, the first American woman to walk in space, was stellar. There is always someone else who can help when your first choice has said no. Be creative and dogged! A lot of people are just looking for an excuse to give up, but a single negative response is not an excuse to give up. It's a call to be a little more strategic and find another way to get what you need.

No doesn't always mean no. It just means no right now. I'm an expert on this one. I can't tell you how many people have initially said no to being interviewed for my books, only to change their minds when I try one more time. Sometimes they don't come around, but I have found that, given a little time and space from the initial request, I can change the minds of about a third of the people when I go back. One approach is to start by saying, "I know you, of all people, can appreciate a little persistence." Sometimes, it's just the nudge they need. Sometimes they won't be nudged.

Just remember, there is *somebody* in power who will help you. You just need to find that somebody.

Use Your Moment Wisely

Before you meet with the person whose help you want, you need to know precisely what it is you need to accomplish by the time the meeting ends. If time is going to be limited, rank things in order of importance. You may be promised an hour and circumstances only give you ten minutes. You can't always begin with what is at the top of your list—some things need a little buildup. I was always careful about that when I was a reporter. If I'd ask the hardest question first, the interview would likely end prematurely. My goal was to make the person feel comfortable and invested. So, think about how you can maximize your time. The time comes when you get your power huddle. Don't advertise your nerves. If you want to be a player, be a player and fit the part.

Go into your meeting as an up-and-coming star who needs mentoring from someone who has already been through the obstacle course. Of course there is a professional power imbalance if you are sitting there with a Fortune 500 CEO, but there is no personal power imbalance, unless you acknowledge it. The other person may have seen and done more than you, and he or she may have acquired more than you. But, he or she has no more right to succeed or enjoy life than you. Your goals matter as much to you as his or hers matter to them. It's one strong, worthy person connecting with another in search of the help that will accomplish something. There was a time when that person was hungry, just like you.

"I still get intimidated by bigger-than-life, famous people," said Ann Tisch, who founded the breakthrough Young Women's Leadership School in Harlem. "Oprah was our keynote speaker for our first graduation. I was totally intimidated by Oprah. My God, it's Oprah Winfrey and I am just little Ann Rubenstein [Tisch] from Kansas City! But, when you are intimidated, fake it. For the five-minute conversation, or the letter you are going to write, or the meeting you are going to attend, just fake it. Put yourself right on their level. You can collapse later." Exactly. Don't cause a major power imbalance by telling the other person, "I'm nervous meeting you." Own your space. That person is no better or no worse than you are. Some people have more money, some people have better jobs, but approach the encounter as one human being to another. Yes, there was a time when Oprah was hungry, too. Her success didn't just land in her lap, and it's not going to land in yours.

Tisch knows that anyone can gain access with the right approach. She certainly appreciates the chance to help others. "The intimidation factor for women is a real factor," she said. "The key is asking for help. You've got to reach down and find your gut. No guts, no glory. One of my mother's lines. The worst thing they can say is no. Take a chance and reach out to someone who does have the visibility or clout and has what you need. People are touched by letters. Reach out and ask for help." If it doesn't go right at first, "You can't be discouraged by one or two no's if, in fact, you believe in what you are doing," she said. Believe, and carry on.

Don't Validate Yourself on Their Dime

Take a couple of minutes to establish common ground and make the other person fall in love with you. That is more important than anything else you do in your meeting. You need to get that person to want to invest in your success. It isn't going to happen if he or she doesn't like, love, or adore you.

But remember, he or she does not want to lose valuable time listening to you cluck on about who you are. You are there to get information. Shut up and get it! If your contact asks specific questions about you, that's one thing. If not, let him or her talk. You don't learn from your contact by wasting time talking about yourself. Engage the other person with what he or she likes to talk about most: himself or herself.

Take notes. If he or she suggests you call somebody, get the person's name or number, and be bold enough to say, "Mind if I drop your name?" That is money in your pocket. While in your meeting, be mindful of the list of things you hoped to accomplish, but don't wed yourself to your list. There may be other valuable things you can learn and gain by letting the other person have a certain amount of control over the conversation. Don't relinquish control completely. That person telling you anecdotes might be a really fun way to spend time together, but it does nothing to move you forward. If he or she veers too far off track, say, "I could talk to you all day. But, I have the feeling you can't talk to me all day, so I'd better make sure I ask you x, y, and z."

Follow Up with Class

Once you've had your moment, make it really count by reviewing your notes and coming up with an action plan that will make the opportunity count. Who are you supposed to contact? What ideas did you get that you need to implement immediately? In the next month? In the next six months? In the next year? Incorporate these ideas into your plans with real goals and deadlines. You have gotten yourself a million bucks worth of free advice. It is worthless unless you do something with it. Come up with a detailed plan that maximizes the worth of your experience.

That night, send a brief thank-you note by e-mail. It should include just a few quick lines to say, "It was great meeting you. You've helped me so much." Then, mail a real thank-you letter that includes a couple of paragraphs that you put in the mail, saying that you really were grateful and that you were willing to make an effort to pass on your gratitude.

In the letter, mention that you will try out some of the person's suggestions, and get back to him or her in a few weeks or a month or two. I'll usually say, "Maybe I can coax you into meeting me for coffee when I have something new to report." The casual approach generally works. The next day, figure out the next person you want to court for help. Start the whole process over, realizing that you are always on a quest for knowledge and insight.

We've all seen stacks of books telling us how women often worry more about relationships than results. We want to be liked. We don't want to ruin a relationship by asking for a favor. We want to seem grateful, not greedy. I cringe every time I hear a friend tell me about landing a new job without haggling over salary. Men expect and respect that basic negotiation. If you don't push for what you deserve, you will be viewed as a softy. You get more respect if you believe in yourself enough to ask for what you want and deserve. What have you got to lose by asking? It's not going to kill you.

No, I didn't ask Cokie Roberts to help me get my book on *Oprah,* but I shouldn't have been so afraid to ask for help. So, if any of you have a direct line to Oprah Winfrey, let me know. Now that I've got another book out, I've got a favor to ask of you.

A MOMENT OF
CHANGE
WITH
Carnie Wilson

Ever since Carnie Wilson was a four year old, she was obsessed with sugar, always craving Hostess Twinkies, cookies, and donuts. The daughter of troubled Beach Boy Brian Wilson and one of the stars of the popular 1990's trio Wilson Phillips, Carnie fought her weight battle in front of the masses. In 1999, at age 31, her much publicized gastric bypass surgery was chronicled live on the Internet, with millions watching.

My high was 300 pounds, and I'm just under 5'4". I wasn't raised in a normal household where your mom and dad go to work and everyone discusses their day at night. I was exposed to a lot of unhealthy things that made me turn to food.

After Wilson Phillips, I was hired to do my talk show. I weighed 240 pounds, and they said, "We love you the way you are." It dawned on me that, maybe, I am meant to be fat. Look at all this positive reinforcement. Someone my size can get on a talk show and be successful! But, after the show was canceled, everything deteriorated. I was in debt, I had no job, and I was gaining a lot of weight. I couldn't stand up because I couldn't take the pressure on my feet. I couldn't breathe while I was sleeping. I was waking up out of breath, coughing, with my heart racing really fast. I'd never heard about sleep apnea, but I had it. My cholesterol was going up, my blood pressure was going up, and there was a voice inside saying, "You are getting ill."

[Beach Boy] Al Jardine asked my sister and me to come on the road and sing as part of Beach Boys, Family and Friends. It was like God saying, "You are going to make some money, but you have to go on the road and perform." I was scared because I didn't have energy and was going onstage weighing 300 pounds. It wasn't comfortable, but I'd get on that stage and totally forget I was fat. I loved every second of it. Then, one morning, I woke up and couldn't move the side of my face. I had Bell's Palsy [facial paralysis]. Looking back, I feel like it was God's way of saying, "Stop. Freeze. Stay still. Look at your life. Look at your health." That's what I did.

I was asked to attend the Million Pound March, and, for God's sake, there really were a million pounds there. It was sad. Here were 200 men and women—mostly women—who were between 300 and 700 pounds, barely walking, huffing and wheezing and red faced, then sitting down, walking then sitting, eating and drinking. And it was so odd. But, everyone had these big smiles on their faces. I didn't relate to one person there. Not one.

I got up there to speak and said, "It's really great to see all your smiling faces, and I'm proud of everyone for standing up for what they believe in their hearts. I just want everyone here to know that I am not proud to be fat and I don't advocate being fat because I think it is unhealthy. I advocate believing in who you are, but I don't want to be overweight." You could have heard a pin drop. The actress Camryn Manheim got up and said, "I just want to say, I'm a size 22 and I'm fucking proud." And, everyone was screaming, "Yea Camryn!" I got up and left.

I did my last concert on my birthday. That was the show when I met my husband. There was this gorgeous guy backstage, who I was immediately pulled to, like a magnet. I fell in love the minute I saw him. During the show, I was jumping around onstage and thought, "Oh my God, the stage is going to break. Don't let the stage break on my birthday." It was a great show. But, I was sweating like a pig. I was so hot and when the concert was over, I got this enormous pain in my right arm. I honestly felt like I was going to have a heart attack. I prayed to God not to let me die. That was the biggest sign I ever had. I went, "Okay, I'm going to have this surgery and I'm going to save my own life."

I lost about 75 pounds in three-and-a-half months. I was down a hundred in six months. And, I started doing more shows with Al, and that was fun because I was thinner and it was easier to perform. I was really confident. Then, one woman said, "My God, you are smaller than your sister." My total loss was 157 pounds. I now weigh 150.

I just want to feel good and make people smile. It's very rewarding when people come up and say I have inspired them. Can you imagine having a hundred people come up and say that you saved their life? My automatic response is that, "*You* did it. *You*. Pat yourself on the back."

For me, the surgery was the best thing I have ever done. But, I was *really* scared.

9.

THE POWER TABOO

Using the Authority You Achieve

I did lunch today with a man who, at 66, reminisced on his storied career. "I loved the power," he said. "It was great. I loved having thousands of employees and a budget of hundreds of millions of dollars. I loved making things happen. Power is *intoxicating*."

He went on and on, and all I could think was, *why do so many men enjoy power, while women make excuses for having it?* Why don't we even say the word out loud? "It's okay to talk about power. It's okay to think about power and it's okay to say, 'Yes, I like having power,' " said Alex Sink, who was once the most powerful woman in American banking before retiring. "I'm very influenced by the man who was the CEO of our bank for years, who loved having power and loved talking about it. He was honest. He said, 'Do I want power? Yes. Do I love having it? Yes.' Power means you are sitting in the chair to effect change in the right way. I always liked being in charge, because I had confidence in my ability to lead the way."

In addition to the altruistic uses of power—to motivate, solve problems, inspire, and make the world better—it's also fine to enjoy power and the trappings that come with it. It's okay to be ambitious and aggressive about your ambitions. Sink sure was, and it put her on the fast track to the top. She hadn't even been at her first banking job a year when she went to her boss and told him she wanted to do more. Her bosses knew she was ambitious and that she was always going to be asking for the next, more powerful challenge. "I'd say, 'Remember how you told me I would be in this job for x amount of time? I've been in this job for almost x amount of time, and I have exceeded expectations and I think it is time for me to be looking for a different challenge,' " she said. A few people tried to hold her back, but usually her bosses told her, "You're right. Let's start looking for another opportunity."

"People are not going to come by your desk and tap you on the shoulder and say, 'You're doing a fantastic job. Go do x, y, or z," Sink said. "Most of the time, the impetus has to come from you."

Getting Your Power

Gail Collins is arguably one of the most powerful women in the nation as editorial page editor at the *New York Times*. However, the first time she used her power was when vying for the editor's position on her college's quarterly magazine. Traditionally, the magazine had co-editors, one male and one female. One of the top male candidates told her that he would like to pair up with her, and if they got it, he'd take care of the graphics side of the magazine and she could have editorial control. She agreed. Then the other top male in the running went into his interview and told the committee that he'd only take the job if he could team up with Collins.

"When I finally got to my interview, they said, 'We have an interesting problem here. We've got two other candidates and they both said they wanted you to be the co-editor. We want you to decide which of them will be your co-editor.' I said, 'Neither. I'd like to do it myself.' They said, 'Okay.' I don't know where exactly it came from. It just popped out. Fortunately both of the guys agreed to be deputy editors and it all worked out okay."

Collins said we have to aggressively manage our paths to power, because no one is going to champion our dreams for us. "Have an idea about where you want to wind up, because normally the people in charge don't have a plan for you. You could very well wind up some place accidentally that you never wanted to be, not because they have an evil plan for you but because they are thinking about other stuff and you sort of fit into the slot right then. You have to have your own vision. Don't presume that anybody else is going to figure out where you ought to be."

Figuring out your own path to success and getting your boss to buy into it is no easy task. We're taught that it's not proper to just come out and say we want power because the traditional notion of power has such a masculine edge to it. There is something that seems, perhaps, unladylike about succeeding in order to attain the mega salaries, enormous offices, and other perks of success. We're allowed to succeed if there is some sort of altruistic motive behind it, but can you imagine a woman saying, "Power corrupts. Absolute power is kinda neat," which is what John Lehman said when he was secretary of the U.S. Navy under Ronald Reagan.

Caroline Turner, who was the senior vice president of Coors before retiring to consult with women on these and other issues, said she appreciated power for what it let her do. "I think we taint the word with notions that power means 'over,' like domination of, rather than strength. It does seem like a dirty word. Women are raised to play games where nobody dominates. There is no boss of dolls. Nobody wins at dolls, and when we get into the corporate world, we seek to share power rather than focus on getting power 'over.' We need to redefine it and have it be okay. We should be comfortable saying, 'I'm powerful.' "

But, we are not comfortable saying it. "We can have an overdeveloped sense of humility that causes us not to take advantage of our influence or power," said AT&T president Betsy Bernard. "Power is the ability to create change through your personal influence. I'm not sure I could even describe what power was during the first decade of my career, even though I used it unconsciously. You use the influence you have wherever you are. You use influence to get things done, you use your network to get things done, and then it gets to the point where you have enough of it that you decide whether or not you have a responsibility to use it for good on a larger stage. That is a conscious decision people make. I do have a significant amount of power and influence, and I not only felt an obligation to use it, but to use it for good." There you have it. Power to achieve, power to influence, power to make a difference.

"In the old days, when women talked about power, it was unfeminine, aggressive, masculine," said Christine Todd Whitman, past governor of New Jersey and former head of the Environmental Protection Agency. "Those were characteristics that set people on edge, made them worry and made them concerned. Now women understand that power is all about your ability to effect change. To get anything done, you have to have some power. I think women seek power as a means to affect an end. It's something that they have an interest and want to change, to reform. It's not just another title or something they want to add to their resume. Then they get in those positions, work hard, and keep moving forward. With some of the men, you will see them kind of sit back and enjoy those things."

Ret. Gen. Claudia Kennedy described discovering several stages of power, authority, and influence during her years in the U.S. Army. She's worked for people who were good about sharing authority, and some who were not. Earlier in her career, when they gave her the authority to do her job, "I didn't feel a surge of power, but a surge of energy and creativity," she said. "It gave me the energy to have the independence to do my work." But, when she didn't get the authority, that energy was sucked right out of her.

When Kennedy became a lieutenant colonel, she learned how power allowed her to influence the bigger system. As a woman who was often the first to do something, she was frequently chosen to serve on committees, like the ones that decided on promotions, training, or special opportunities. "I loved it," she said, "because I really wanted to be in on shaping the future. I was able to influence the Army because I was in on the selection process of the leaders. Knowing who they were and what they stood for made a difference." For example, if she knew a particular candidate was a bigot, she'd vote against him. Others in power might not have seen the individual's racial biases as cause for derailing a career, but Kennedy knew that she could use her influence to win one for Liberty. Again, the altruism. Once you get power, create a better world.

Why do women frequently link the concepts of power and altruism together?

"What's wrong with that?" Tampa mayor Pam Iorio asked. Nothing! Power helps us to help others, I've been told repeatedly. When we find ourselves in the world of power, we can make a better world. And, that's great. But, if we want to be in the game, we've got to get in the game. If we don't play tough, we'll be run over. Sometimes, altruism doesn't cut it, although I will never minimize it as a motive. We've got to be bold enough to say we want to win and tough enough to face the consequences of sometimes doing unpopular things. Then we have to push forward with our vision. Women of power say, "I want to win," rather than, "I wish I could make this happen," or, "I think I will try this," or "Wouldn't it be nice." We have to say, "I'm going forward with this. I'm going to do it."

Using Your Power

The most articulate explanation of power—and our odd relationship with it—came from Alexa Canady, the first woman and African American to become a neurosurgeon. "You don't have any power if you don't use it," she told me. "What is power if it is not used? It is a meaningless concept. If someone is unwilling to exert power, they have no power. Power is not something that is out there. It is something you say, 'I will use this to obtain what I want.' Other people know if you are going to fight. If they know you won't, you have no power."

One thing to remember is that there is power and there is authority. They are not the same things. You can have all the authority in the world, but if your people don't buy in, you have no power. Some people have the innate ability to change everything around them without the title, position, or authority. People listen to or follow them, which makes them powerful. They have influence. Influence is true power.

"Because I said so" may have been good enough for your mother, but it's not good for anyone else. Those who count on raw authority to lead have trouble lining up followers. You can force people to obey, but not to respect. You can order them to act, but not believe. You have ten times as much influence when you let your people feel their personal power and give them chances to expand it. Hear them. Include them. They have every right to want to be involved—to count—in the success of your vision. If you can inspire others to want to do the things you need done, you have real power. And respect. Respect them, and they'll respect you. You don't order that; it just happens.

What makes you a better leader? Is it what you order people to do, or what you teach and inspire others to accomplish? What you know, or what the people you surround yourself with know? What is the deal with those people who get hung up on being the holder of all knowledge, the seer of all vision? You will be so much more successful if you want your people to be successful, and care enough about them to let them grow beyond the job definitions that make your life convenient. If you just give someone the tools to do a job, they'll do the job. But, if you give them the tools to grow and succeed, they will propel your success forward.

"People are longing for leadership," said Arianna Huffington, the nationally syndicated columnist and author of nine books. "Leadership for me is about looking around the corner and seeing the crises that are imminent and dealing with them before the Titanic hits the iceberg. For me, that's a great quality of leadership. It's also being able to carry the people with you. You have to carry a critical mass with you to get things done. You need to communicate. Be clear about what you are communicating, and don't take things personally when you encounter resistance."

"Don't be timid about your power. Use it. Risk disapproval," Huffington said. "The most important thing is that you know life goes on, and no one conflict is going to ruin you. I am criticized for being aggressive, being driven—characteristics that nobody questions in a man but constantly question in a woman. It is important that women who have the passion to lead are able to do that without holding back. If you have this burning desire to change things and make a difference, don't hold back. We all have different destinies."

Huffington reminds herself of what her mother taught her—that courage is the knowledge of what is not to be feared. "Very often we are afraid of our own shadows," Huffington said. "It's not like anything will happen to us."

Sharing Your Power

Success and power are not finite qualities, so don't be so foolish to think that you need to hoard them for yourself. There is enough success for everyone, so share it. And, make an effort to share it with other women. Other women should not be your rivals just because you think there is a limited amount of success available to women and you want it. The more power one women has, the more power all women will have. The way to make power grow is to share the power you have. Be human about it.

"I think people make a very big mistake by not showing their human sides. More often than not, if people can see the sensitive side of women in business, they relate better to them," said Janet L. Robinson, president and incoming CEO of The New York Times Publishing Company. "They realize we have frailties just like they do, and it really strengthens relationships. There are women in business and politics and the legal profession, or physicians who are arrogant, and many of them got to where they are now by constantly fighting to get there. And I think women of my age had a harder time than women a bit younger than I am right now. And in light of that, I think that arrogance grew—that thick skin developed primarily because they were constantly fighting to reach that level they are within the companies."

We're on our way, said Marie Wilson, president of the Ms. Foundation,

Women in Charge

Why is the notion of a woman president so radical in the United States? Worldwide, women have gained so much stature as leaders around the world. As I write this, the presidents of Finland, Ireland, Indonesia, Latvia, Panama, the Philippines, and Sri Lanka are all women, as are the prime ministers of New Zealand and Bangladesh. In the past, women have been president or prime minister of the following countries: Great Britain, Argentina, Canada, Switzerland, France, Turkey, Central African Republic, Dominica, Guyana, Haiti, Iceland, India, Israel, Lithuania, Malta, Netherlands Antilles, Nicaragua, Norway, Portugal, and Rwanda.

and current president of the White House Project. "The only power women have traditionally been granted in this society is the power of mothers, of givers, of public utility. When we really have power and we exert it, others get uncomfortable. But, they are getting more used to it because we are at the tipping point. All over the world, people are getting more accustomed to women having power and wanting women to have power because they trust what women will do with it."

Women use power every day. We've become clever on our path to get things done. We have strategies to acquire and use the resources that help us to be effective with our power. "It's just getting the resources, whether those are capital or intellectual or human that let you do what you need to do in the world," Wilson continued. "It's not that people don't want to work for women. They want to work for people who have resources to get them what they want."

The Price of Power

As women, we have the desire to be beloved. But, the person who is most powerful is not always the one who is adored. Exerting power by changing the rules, hiring, or firing can make enemies. If you exert your power, you may face painful consequences. Some people might resent you, think you made lousy decisions, try to undermine you, or even attempt a coup. But, when you don't exert your power, the consequences are likely to be even worse. You'll struggle to implement your vision. Others will dismiss you as a lightweight and further minimize your effectiveness. Power gives you an opportunity to lead, but lead wisely. Build respect. Don't intimidate, unless you have to. You are a part of the team, too.

One time, I watched a top manager yell at his department heads, "I demand to be respected!" Well, you can demand that someone be at work at 9 a.m. You can demand that he or she do certain tasks before they leave for the day. You can insist that they meet with you. But there is *nothing* you can do to force someone to respect you, or like you, think you are smart, or agree with what you are doing. Nothing, except be worthy. You can have all the authority in the world, but without the respect that you have to earn from others, you have no power. Your people will drive your success, so let them enjoy theirs. Don't stand out front and tell them when, where, and how to march behind you. Stand beside them and bring them with you.

Sometimes, we need to learn to turn up the volume on our internal power meter, and sometimes, we need to turn it down. That's why power is so tricky. We've got to want it, have it, and use it. But we have to use it carefully so we don't undermine our efforts by turning everybody off. That's especially tough for women. "Women live in a flat organization. They share power equally," said author and international workplace consultant Pat Heim. Her *Hardball for Women: Winning at the Game of Business* is the most enlightening book on gender issues at work that I have ever read. "Men live hierarchically, and they are always trying to climb up the ladder, whether it is at work or in golf," she said. "When a woman does this, the other women will zap her. This is actually biologically and chemically driven in women."

A woman who stands out might not hear the snide "Who does she think she is" chorus in the background, but, way too often, it's there. "Women don't want one woman to be in charge," Heim said. "We share power equally. It's what I call the 'power dead even' rule. If a woman behaves as if she has more power, she will be completely zapped by other women." Heim told me to imagine her arrogantly saying, "I am Dr. Heim." It wouldn't go over well. But, she said, men do that all the time. A man will think nothing of saying, "I don't know if you have heard, but I got promoted to vice president," she explained. Beyond that, we are often befuddled by the different rules and expectations that exist for women at work. "The research on aggressiveness among executives is that both male and female executives must be aggressive," Heim said. "But, men can display aggressiveness in a wide variety of ways. I've seen men pound on tables in meetings. If a woman did that, they'd say, 'Call the psych hospital. She's lost it.'"

It is disconcerting to see what happens to the woman who finally gets to the top and displays the aggressiveness she needed to get and stay there, Heim said. Who is the first to attack her? It's not the men, but the other women who will dismiss her as a bitch. "The reality is, if she doesn't display that behavior, she isn't going to be able to stay there and fight for the other women in the organization," Heim said. "It is a really tough, tough fine line."

Several years ago, she met with about 20 senior women from top organizations. She was astounded by the number of women in the group who had suffered nervous breakdowns. Bravely and honestly, they talked about it. Heim recounted their shared experiences. "You have to do one thing to get promoted, and when you do it, you get zapped for it," she explained. "I mean, is there any way to win here? You do just what your male counterparts want, but you are the bad guy or the bitch. Here you are a female with all this oxytocin running around and you need some people you are close to, who you can connect with, and they see you as a bitch. Where do you go?" The key, Heim found, was for women to build alliances with other women. "You *have* to. And then, you have to move in concert. This is a really difficult thing for women.

Projecting Power

* Tell yourself you deserve your job and your success.
* Stop wasting stress on trying to prove your worthiness. Do your job.
* Make peace with your fear of public speaking. People in power have to do it. Act as if you are powerful. Walk, talk and behave with confidence.
* Dress for the job you want, not the one you have.
* Watch your temper and your tears. They rarely work in a woman's favor.
* Watch your words and expressions. A joke, a slight criticism, an abrupt e-mail—even an unintended smirk can be so misinterpreted that you ruin a connection forever.
* Read the headlines every day so you have something to talk about with just about anybody.
* If you wait for a pause to make a point in a meeting, you're going to miss your moment again and again. Study how men interrupt or jump in one second before the previous speaker has finished.
* Know the difference between being accommodating and submissive.
* Play to your strengths.

Let's say you have a cadre of women who think there is a problem, and they are willing to do something about it, but need a leader. Women don't do well with women who are leaders. Once the leader starts telling other women what the plan is, then *she* is the problem," Heim said.

Ah, the oxytocin factor. Oxytocin has been called as the "cuddle hormone." It stimulates everything from contractions in labor to the delivery of milk for breastfeeding, orgasms, and the need to bond. It is powerful, and in stressful situations especially, it drives our need to connect to other women. But when women turn on us, what are we to do? It's lonely at the top, especially if you are a woman. If I ask a group of women if they have been knifed in the back by men, they have to think about it. If I ask if they've been sabotaged by women, the response is immediate, furious, and painful. That doesn't mean men haven't sabotaged us, but when women do it, we remember.

"We have not had culturally approved ways to deal with other women except as rivals for a limited supply of the goodies or men," said author Dr. Christiane Northrup. "But most of it is our internalized distrust of other women. It comes from the zero-sum model that says there is only so much to go around, and if I take mine, there will be less for you. It also comes from valuing men over women. Women are taught from the earliest age to jockey for position instead of seeing the value of their relationships with women. I'm thrilled we are finally shedding light on this dark area. It is time. Women are never going to get anywhere as a gender and will never reach equality with men if we are still fighting with one another."

The Illusion of Power

An immaculately dressed businessman came to pick up his Lincoln at the Budget Rent-a-Car counter in Tampa, while I was also in line. This man exuded confidence and power, and I wondered why this CEO-type hadn't called for a limo or just sent his personal assistant to pick up the car from that tiny rental office near the university. He made small talk with the clerk, but seemed impatient about getting his car.

"I'm sorry," the clerk finally said, "but your credit card has been rejected. Do you have another that might have room for $250 on it?"

"They told me on the phone I only needed $100!" the man shouted, quite irate.

"I'm sorry, it's $250," the clerk said.

Without another word, the man stormed out the front door and got into his real car, a beat up, rusted Skylark that had been issued sometime when I was still in college. He peeled away, leaving a cloud of exhaust behind the car. It would have been humorous, had it not been so sad. Obviously, this man needed to create a good impression for some reason, but couldn't pull it off without the Lincoln. With the Lincoln, he would be whomever we could imagine him being.

The illusion of power counts. People feel confident about you when you feel confident about yourself. They believe in your power when you feel it yourself. You have so much power over the impression you create, yet, how can you be worried about looking or acting powerful if you are set on being authentic to who you are?

"I know we aren't supposed to think these things in the new feminist millennium," said former Texas governor Ann Richards. "But how you dress also says a lot about what you think about yourself. If you want to be taken seriously, then dress like you take yourself seriously. Women who come in with a bunch of chains around their neck, earrings dangling off their ears—it tells you something. It tells you that this is a frivolous person. And that you have deliberately adorned yourself in a way to cause a distraction from what you have to say."

As someone who has rarely gotten it right when it comes to fashion at work, at home, or anywhere else, I wasn't sure how to react to what Richards said. This book is about being yourself in a go-along-to-get-along world. How can we be ourselves if we are so focused on our images? Well, there comes a point when we have to acknowledge the way the world works—and doesn't. We really can't be our most comfortable self at all times and expect to be effective. If we could, about 90 percent of us would show up at work dressed for playtime, rather than business. But, there's an old saying: "Don't dress for the job you have, dress for the job you want." And, there is truly something to it. We shouldn't have to lose ourselves to somebody else's fashion rules or expectations, but if our effectiveness is diluted by bad image planning, we should make a conscious choice about what we will and won't do.

"I always wear very simple, plain clothes," Richards explained. "I don't wear flowered things; I don't wear big stripes or big plaids. I wear solid-colored pant suits. I usually wear a shirt that is the same color as the suit, and jewelry. I will wear some very simple earrings, something that fits flat to my ear. I will wear a good ring, a good watch. I might wear a bracelet, but if I do, it doesn't have things hanging off of it that jingle. I don't carry the kind of purse that, when you set it down, clanks or bangs. No over-the-shoulder strap. I want it clear that I'm here to work and I'm here for business. This is not a style show. I wear black, I wear navy blue, occasionally I might wear a real bright jacket, but it's going to be a very simple, businesslike cut."

So, there I was, getting fashion advice from Richards, and my mind flashed to the photo I ran across of a 24-year-old Fawn Germer reporting on a crash on a bridge in Jacksonville. There I was in jeans and (cringe) flip-flops. I asked Richards if she always had an instinct about such matters, and she said no. She didn't even run for office until she was in her late 40s. "I paid attention to people who, if I liked the way they looked and acted, I tried to emulate. When I was young, there weren't any mentors. Literally, there weren't women in leadership. But I went to an event in Houston for the International Women's Year, and all the first ladies were there—Miss Ford, Miss Johnson–Lady Bird, Miss Carter. And, I just remember those four and they had these beautiful colors on. So, when I was in public office, I always wore a bright colored, simple jacket because it differentiated me from the men."

It's all in how you look. How you walk. How you act.

Protecting Your Power

One of the most brilliant and dedicated women mentors I have ever known has just freed herself from a boss who did everything he could to put her in her place. He took away her authority, assigned her to menial tasks, put her down, and held her back. And this is a woman of such brains and warmth for whom you or I would only expect great things.

But she, like most of us, encountered a tormentor who wanted to take away her power. Because she had no possibility of getting help from the men above her boss, I told her she had four options:

1. Be miserable.

2. Make peace with it.

3. Start looking for something else.

4. Walk off without another job.

All are valid options. You can stay, or you can go. But it is your choice; you are never as powerless as you think. And, when you encounter a power vampire who tries to suck your energy and verve right out of you, remember this: they are just players you allow in your life, and it is your choice how long you will give them control over you. Her boss took charge just as the economy tanked and everyone in her area seemed to be looking for work. It took more than a year of networking and pounding every inch of pavement to find a great fit for her passion and talent. In the meantime, she still had to endure a daily dose of abuse from that mean little man who apparently made himself feel bigger by bringing others down. Eventually she found a new job and she became her happy self again. Someone may torment you for now, but it won't last forever—unless you let it.

In our desperation to maintain control, we often forget that we always have the ultimate say, especially when others take active steps to make us feel powerless.

Look back over every boss you have ever had in your life. At the time, they had great authority over you. But, the minute you quit, they had none. You had all the power over you. You are the only constant in your life.

It's pretty enlightening when you look back on the situations or people who made you crazy. Why would you stay around for continued abuse? Look your fears in the eye and know that you are marketable, determined, *and* powerful. No matter how much someone has affected your self-esteem, you've got to believe in yourself. There are jerks in the world who sometimes have great power and control over our security and our futures. But generally, they are in our lives because we give them permission to be in our lives. You can always "fire" your boss. You probably haven't seen the last jerk in your life, but they do come and they do go. Some of them will trip up and suffer payback for their misdeeds. Mean people do fall down, but they don't always do it in front of us or when it's most opportune to us. I don't gloat watching someone like that take a dive. Well, not too much. No use attracting bad energy.

Finding Your Internal Power When Someone Has Pushed You Down

* There is only one reason you will remain in a powerless situation for an extended period of time, and that is choice. You can choose to be miserable or choose to make changes.
* In life, we have our mentors and our tormentors. The tormentors never last in our lives—unless we choose to keep them there. If you have to endure a bad boss, bad life partner, or bad colleagues, that is your choice.
* You can always walk out. Smart women survive. I've seen friends max out their credit cards and face bankruptcy, but ultimately, they found great success again. There will be obstacles. Smart women survive. Smart women survive. Smart women survive.
* Sometimes things change when we don't do anything, but don't count on it. Sometimes out tormentors leave their jobs, get promoted, or get demoted. At some point, there will be some sort of a change. But, it's not worth losing five years of your life to being miserable. And, you can't always count on things changing for the better. Sometimes you lose one jerk for an even bigger jerk.
* Stop killing yourself to impress someone when it becomes obvious it will never happen. Do the minimum for awhile while you come up with your plan.
* If things go bad in one area of your life, nurture another area. Do something adventurous. Be with people you love. Whatever is giving you trouble is only one part of what is going on in your world.

The Power of Altruism

I started this chapter talking about how women feel the need to justify their acquisition of power by saying it allows them to do so many good things. That doesn't need to be your reason for acquiring power, but once you've got it, do good things.

We are beyond the point of needing an excuse to enjoy the possibility of what our power can allow us to do. Go ahead. Enjoy it. But, use it with a conscience. I recently got to know a woman executive who was making big headlines, embroiled in a corporate scandal. I don't know if she should have been hugged or indicted; I can't vouch for what she did or didn't do. But, that woman knew real fear—not because she was going to lose her title or her office, not because she was being savaged in the media, and not because the career she'd fought so hard to build was very likely dead. I saw a woman in real fear of going to prison, being cut off from her husband and children. She'd been driven to get the title, the power, and the money because she'd been taught that those things were the symbols of success. Faced with the prospect of losing it all, she learned the simplest lesson of all: it's not what you have, but who you are. You don't have to rise to the top and get yourself a seven-figure income to figure that out. The things she was most terrified of losing were the things most of us already have.

Do we use altruism as an excuse for power? Maybe. But, so what?

I recently read news that a female top executive was poised to receive more than $50 million in bonuses while simultaneously laying off 15,000 people in her company. It made me sick. The bad publicity, of course, killed the bonus, but she did walk away that year with $10 million. I've been disgusted by so many male CEOs who set that norm for behavior, and while I'm sure there are plenty of women who would argue that I don't have the right to hold the bar higher for women than men, I do. *We know better. We can do better.* Just because we get the power doesn't mean we have to use it the way it has always been used. Sure, we can be greedy, selfish, and nasty, but why? We live in a beautiful world that still needs improvement. Improve it! Do better than it's always been done. Lead.

Then you'll know *real* power.

A MOMENT OF
HONOR
WITH
Coleen Rowley

Why didn't FBI leadership listen—and do something—when the Minneapolis bureau reported that Zacarias Moussaoui, a French-Moroccan, had signed up for lessons at a local flight school, inquiring about learning to fly a jumbo jet? Moussaoui, the only person charged as a conspirator in the 9-11 disasters, became a symbol of our intelligence forces not connecting the critical dots. If FBI leadership had listened, could 9-11 have been prevented or minimized?

Coleen Rowley, a career attorney for the FBI, knew the hard questions had to be asked. If operations didn't change, would it happen again? She was one of the first people inside the FBI to publicly question that agency's role in 9-11, and she became famous for penning a frank, concerned memo to FBI director Robert Mueller detailing the agency's shortfalls.

She thought it was just a memo. It was history. It marked a watershed moment that highlighted intelligence community, and her subsequent testimony on Capitol Hill was unforgettable. Columnists took shots at her words and her appearance, but, that didn't matter. Time magazine named Rowley Person of the Year for 2002, along with the whistleblowers from Enron and WorldCom. She's a legend.

I don't like the term "whistleblower." I don't like that idea of being someone who runs around blowing a whistle like an alarmist or disgruntled person.

None of this was planned. I wrote my memo because I didn't want to forget what to say. I'm not that good verbally. In the Minneapolis bureau, we really thought that the hierarchy at the FBI had not told the full story, and that it had been glossed over and skewed. The whole point of being in the FBI is that you are enforcing the law, and the slightest hint of a lack of integrity is really a problem. They drilled that into us. The appearance of unprofessionalism, the appearance of something less than top ethical behavior is a problem in the FBI, off duty, or on.

But, it seemed to me that the public statements about what happened before 9-11 were not correct.

When I delivered the memos, my knees were so weak. It was so strongly worded, and taking something like that to the director was, of course, scary. Handing anything like that to your top boss is scary, and since I have done it, it's probably gotten scarier. Here I am, a triathlete, but I was shaking when I dropped it off. But, I had to follow through.

I was scared about testifying. I had drafted a statement about some of the main endemic problems facing the FBI but did not have enough time to really prepare very well. But the members of the committee, their remarks were all very nice. Maybe overly nice. Retired agents were critical of me. They said the senators asked me softball questions, like it was a setup and the senators were trying to use it for political gain. Like I just fell into the trap. I think former agents have a lot of pride in having worked for the FBI. That's usually a good thing, but can become bad if you don't admit to any need for improvement. They were seeing me as criticizing the FBI. The criticism, alone, is what they objected to. For some of them, the fact that I was female might have been a factor because many of them had been around prior to 1972 when the FBI didn't even allow females to become agents.

The night before I testified, I met Director Mueller in his office. He didn't discuss what I was going to say, and I thought this was quite unique. I was getting to speak without having been previewed. That never happens in the FBI.

Most of the media coverage was favorable, and I knew that was some form of protection. But, the media are fickle. We've had cases where, one day, you are hailed as a hero, and the next, you are the villain. They are always looking for new angles on stories, and if you count on the media as some form of protection, you are sadly mistaken. A couple of female commentators made remarks about what I wore and about my glasses. I know I'm not a fashionable dresser and even I didn't like my glasses. But, I'm not the type of person who goes out and hunts for things because of fashion. I wait for things to break. I wore those glasses all summer, and finally they broke when I was on vacation. Then I bought more modern-looking glasses. But, if people criticize me for not being fashionable, it doesn't bother me. That's not what I'm into.

I still don't see that I did anything and I kind of regret that it has become viewed in this way. This was really something that was more than myself. It was my whole office. I don't know that we could have prevented 9-11. Maybe there was some chance, if all the stars had lined up correctly. Maybe we could have made it less than it was.

My message is this: When you find yourself in a bad situation, do something. Do the right thing. Tell the truth. If you make a mistake, own up to it. I would love to be aside from that and not have been a part of all this personally.

When you find yourself in these situations, try to think back to your moral compass and determine what is the right thing to do. There are some gray areas and real ethical dilemmas. But, as hard as it may be, take that first step, then follow through. A lot of people take the path of least resistance. Don't go along with the crowd. Do the right thing.

NOTE: *Rowley is required to note she was interviewed in her personal capacity and not on behalf of the FBI.*

10.

IT'S NOT ALL ABOUT YOU

Gaining Perspective on the Actions of Others

"JUST *send* me the two paragraphs!" SLAM!

For the first time in all my years of journalism, an editor screamed at me, then slammed down the phone. All I'd wanted to do was add two paragraphs to a legally sensitive column, and I wanted to do it myself so the facts stayed in context. What had I done to provoke this anger? I was leaving the next day on a vacation, and would have a whole week to torture myself wondering what I'd done wrong. I was sure the problem was me.

When I got back from my trip, I e-mailed the top editor, a woman who does her share of self-evaluation, and asked for some input. Had I been too strident? This episode turned into one of the most important awakenings I've ever had.

"What happened is not about you," she said. "It's about him."

The world does not revolve around me. My perspective is not the only perspective. The way other people act and react may—or may not—have to do with me. I'd spent a week of vacation fretting about that guy hanging up on me when, minutes before, he'd hung up on another writer, too.

It had nothing to do with me? How was that possible?

What Do They Think of Me?

All the smirks, criticism, outbursts, and attitudes that we feel certain have everything to do with us often have absolutely nothing to do with us. I spent years thinking that my bosses were fixated on me whenever they glanced in my direction. I was not a paranoid person at all, except when it came to work. At work, I thought everything was all about me, and that had to impact my effectiveness. How can you present new ideas, ask for promotions, or even comfortably crack a good joke when you think someone is displeased with you? If you feel someone is watching your every move, how will you ever relax enough to be yourself and succeed on your own terms? I'm not the only one who has fueled my own insecurities by the all-about-me perspective. If it's been all about you, consider this as your awakening.

Before you start to think someone is mad, disappointed, frustrated, irritated, aggravated, perturbed, dissatisfied, disillusioned, upset, anxious, worried, disturbed, or anything else in relation to you or something you have done, run through the possibilities. Is the person just having a

Getting a Little Perspective

This exercise can be enlightening and fun—if you have the guts to try it. If you are friends with colleagues or supervisors, why not get a little input on what is real and what is not? If you are wondering about an old situation, say, "Remember when (fill in the blank with an incident that made you especially nervous) happened? I'm just curious. What do you think was going on?" If it is a current situation, say, "Hey, I'm trying to get a little perspective about what is going on with (fill in the blank). How do you see the situation?"

Asking can be stressful, even if you are looking at something that happened years ago, but if you have the courage to ask, you just might enlighten yourself with valuable perspective. If you see the value in knowing when you get it right or wrong, have the courage to ask for that perspective. It is powerful.

tough day? Maybe there is a family member who is ill. Maybe somebody bounced a check. Maybe the kids are in trouble at school again. Maybe her husband left her for another woman. Maybe his wife can't stand him anymore. Maybe he's in trouble with his boss. Maybe the contractor vanished. Maybe the bank is foreclosing. Maybe she had a flat tire on the way to work.

"We think we did something wrong. It's our fault, it's our fault, it's all our fault," said national radio host Laura Ingraham. "You have to step outside of yourself, see the world through other people's eyes and see some decisions are made that have absolutely nothing to do with whether you are great at what you do or are failing at what you do."

When Elizabeth Roberts was managing editor at *Working Woman,* she noticed the "it's all about me complex" in action. "If the editor-in-chief came in and was preoccupied and was short in her answers or her attention, junior staffers would take it personally, like they had affronted her." said Roberts, now a senior editor at *Martha Stewart Living.* "They couldn't look at the bigger picture. They personalized it: 'Oh my God, she's mad at me!' They'd come to me for reassurance or some explanation, and the explanation was that the editor-in-chief had a big meeting that afternoon. It had nothing to do with them. It was enlightening to see that personalization of things."

"At some point, you have to determine what really is about you and what isn't, but if you constantly ask if you've done something wrong, you'll come off as immature or self-involved," Roberts said. Instead, she suggested we all think more critically about the multitude of explanations that exist. "Look at the bigger picture," she advised. "Look for reasons beyond your own self for why things are happening."

New York Times editorial page editor Gail Collins said she learned that trick at home. "My husband will be in a bad mood and I'll theorize what it is that I said or did then I realize it could be the ball team losing or something that happened at his work. We always tend to put ourselves in the center of what's going on."

Once you stop doing that, you can watch your stress level slide. A board member was making communication tense for Jane Smith, CEO of Business and Professional Women/USA. "At first, I read things the wrong

way," Smith said. "I took it that we were not living up to our performance." Smith later learned that difficulties in that board member's life
were affecting her attitude. "Everything we are is all rolled up into one.
When I work with you, I am getting everything of you—not just the discussion we are having. I am getting everything that happened yesterday,
with everybody else, too."

Laura Ingraham recalled when her television show was canceled on
MSNBC. Her first instinct was that it was, of course, all about her. Then
she stepped back and looked at what she'd accomplished. The show was
good. It had a good following. "It took me a week to get over my dejec-
tion about it," she said. "This is a business. Sometimes, you get caught in

How to Know When It Really *Is* All about You

Getting the real skinny involves a delicate balance of asking questions
of yourself—and others. Start with a little self-evaluation:

1. Are you being treated differently from your peers? In what ways? Is it
   severe?
2. Do you have a history of being overly nervous about what others
   think of you or of overreacting to what people say?
3. When was the last time you received input from the person who is
   making you nervous? What happened?
4. Has this person been consistent in dealing with you? How have things
   changed? What may have sparked the change in attitude?
5. Have you received any overt criticism or signals that you are in trouble?
6. Have you asked what gives? What kind of response did you get?
7. If your fears are true, how will the dissatisfied person's concerns impact you? What is the worst-case scenario? What is a more realistic
   appraisal of the potential fallout?
8. If it's not all about you, what else might it be about? How well do you
   know the person who seems to have a problem with you? Are there
   other issues bothering this person? Is he or she the one that is really
   under fire?

the spokes and run over. Lineups change, and it's not all personal. It's not all about me. It's money, and a lot of other factors. There might be politics involved. Whatever. It is bigger than me. Bigger than my show. It wasn't an indictment of my worth as a television host. It's bigger than me." Coming to that realization takes a little experience and some personal evolution.

"Just relax," said Kathleen Carroll, executive editor of the Associated Press. "You may think somebody is in there thinking about you every minute of every day, but it ain't happening."

I have to laugh about my own worries. All those years, sitting in the newsroom, seeing the big bosses behind the windows of their glass offices. Talk about paranoia-inducing environments! Every single time they glanced out the glass office window in my direction, I just knew they were thinking about me—either about how well I was doing, or how I wasn't measuring up. At some point, I got smart and made sure my desk was nowhere near a glass window or walkway. I shared my insecurity with a mid-level editor who explained, quite matter of factly, that the bosses did not have time to be so worried about me because, she laughed, "They are in there thinking about *me*." What were they *really* thinking? They were probably wondering whether they were going to get Chinese or subs for lunch. That's what they do in those glass offices; they make lofty decisions.

Was I Really Slighted?

Somebody doesn't answer an e-mail. Or someone with caller ID doesn't answer the phone when you know he or she is home. You invite them over for dinner but never get invited to their house. You drop by for a visit but aren't asked inside.

The list of slights can go on and on. The unanswered e-mail? Maybe she gets several hundred a day. Maybe he has someone checking it for him. The phone that isn't answered? Maybe he is in the shower. Perhaps the ringer is off. The dinner invite? He hates cooking. She has bad manners. When you stopped by? The house was a mess. There are a million possible scenarios for every slight. Don't assume anything!

I once contacted a woman who ran an interesting Internet site and casually said I might interview her sometime in the future. About a week later, I got a very long e-mail from her wondering how she'd insulted me. She dissected every word of our prior correspondence, apologizing for being pushy and aggressive. There was a real reason why I hadn't called her for an interview. I'd forgotten. Sometimes, good people unintentionally do rude things. Don't look for slights.

What If It Really *Is* All about Me?

It's too bad it is so hard to know when it *is* about us. People aren't all that honest, and plenty of men and women will do just about anything to avoid confrontation. I've always said the contents of an employee evaluation should never surprise the employee, but evaluations are frequently filled with surprises. Why? Because managers are often loathe to bring up a touchy situation directly. Or, if they bring it up, we might not quite hear the concerns the way they were meant to be heard. We can ask how we are doing, but how many times are we going to get a thoughtful, honest response? If we keep asking, "How am I doing?" or, "Are you mad at me?" aren't we advertising our insecurities?

Alexa Canady, the first woman and the first African-American neurosurgeon, spent plenty of time dealing with medical students who were trying to decode what was really behind faculty decisions at Wayne State University, where Canady was on the faculty. "Medical students are a particularly paranoid lot," she said. "You are always trying to read the faculty. What do they mean? What are they doing? Something happens in scheduling and the students say 'The faculty is trying to get us.' But, they weren't even thinking about the students." She'd advise them, "As a young person, you don't appreciate the pressures on the person above you and the pressures they have in terms of their own career building. A lot of things don't have anything to do with you."

Sometimes, there is no great conspiracy. Sometimes, the boss decides to send your co-worker to a conference instead of you because your co-worker walked into the office just as he was thinking about who he'd send. Sometimes, you are handed an ugly schedule, not as retribution, but because the boss actually trusts you to do a good job at a time when the rest of the staff isn't stellar, or because she needs somebody to work that shift. Your friend might have gotten a bigger raise than you because her evaluation came earlier in the budget year, when there was more money in the pot. A colleague might snap at you because he's got financial problems, or a sick relative, or even plain ol' indigestion. If you are in the wrong, find out and right it.

Be honest with yourself and ask the hard questions. Is there something you need to do to change your situation or the perception of you? Do it. If someone is angry or critical because of something you have done—and you really are in the wrong—address it and fix it. Own it and do better. We all have periods in our life when we could do better. Recognize those moments and take action.

Sometimes it helps to realize that the leader is often under as much pressure as the follower, the manager is often as worried as the employee, and the decision-maker is as frantic as the person impacted by the decision. The paranoia we feel in the workplace and, in certain social situations, is amplified for us as women, because we are so concerned about being liked and appreciated. "Women are socialized from the very beginning to care about how other people feel and internalize that empathy," said Yolanda Moses, president of the American Association for Higher Education and the former president of City College of New York. "In a work environment, where you are a manager or a leader, a lot of people may be directing barbs at you that are not directed at *you,* but are directed at the leader who is that impersonal person who is making unpopular decisions. You have to get a tough skin on the outside, even though on the inside you care about people. Act on your emotions and feelings from an ethical place that is consistent so, whether someone likes you or not is immaterial if you are making the right decision. You have to learn that early on, or you will get caught in crossfires, conundrums, or hurt feelings. Once you feel hurt and can't trust people, you can't be an effective leader. If you start to withdraw, you can't be effective."

Did I Really Do Something Wrong?

We often make negative assumptions about what is really going on because of our own life issues. "Anytime anyone is mean to me, I think it is all about me," said playwright Eve Ensler. "And I go back to the place where I was treated badly most days of my life. I thought it was all about me. I've gotten to a point where I'm much faster to think it's not about me. Or, sometimes it is about me. I try to live in a way that if I am wrong and make a mistake, I promptly admit it. I try to make amends as soon as I can. I don't care about saying I'm sorry. I'm fine about saying I'm sorry. I don't need to be right. I would rather things get better."

Just make sure that when you apologize, you've done something wrong. Men are more prone to blaming their difficulties on anything or anyone but themselves, said international management consultant Pat Heim, who specializes in gender issues. A project that flopped might be explained away by saying, "Well, I didn't have the time to do it right," or, "I didn't have the support I needed," or, "I didn't get enough information." See? It's generally somebody or something else that created the problem. Not a lot of introspection there.

Us women? We love to blame ourselves. "Men will attribute screw-ups to external factors," said Heim. "Women will attribute the screw-up to themselves: 'I should have tried harder,' 'I must have done something wrong,' 'I must have pissed this guy off.' So, as a result, women find themselves in the wrong because we've put ourselves there. I refer to a cartoon where the first frame has a woman trying to get her pants zipped up. Her caption says, 'I have got to go on a diet.' The next frame is a man trying to get his zipped up, and the caption is, 'Something is wrong with these pants.' It's what I call pointing the finger out, versus pointing the finger in."

When things go right? Well, just watch the guys. They puff up their chests and take credit for their brilliance and finesse. They never say, "Oh, it was nothing." They say, "It was everything! The greatest thing ever accomplished in the history of humankind!" When women do well, we minimize our achievement by saying how hard we tried, by noting that the achievement wasn't that difficult, or by saying how lucky we were that everything worked out. "We don't see the dynamic until somebody points it out and then it's, 'Oh! I can't believe it. I do that all the time!' " Heim explained.

No wonder we are so nervous when it comes to interacting with others. We don't even put ourselves on sound footing. We've got to find ways to acknowledge our worth and really know our strength, so it's not so easy to deflate our self-confidence. Think about it: if we were more secure in our own abilities, we wouldn't be so frantic about what others think about us.

Am I Nervous for Good Reason?

I can tell you that it's not all about you a thousand times, but the workplace has changed so much that it is easy to see why you're skeptical. It wasn't long ago when we joked about Big Brother in fictional terms, but our world has truly given life to Big Brother. We *are* being watched. There are surveillance cameras just about everywhere we go, and the government has countless ways to keep tabs on what we do. The Big Brother mentality has really impeded our ability to live and breathe in the workplace. The corporate world now actively takes steps to spy on us. No wonder we are nervous.

You never really know if employers are reading your e-mail. By law, they have the right to do so. Employers also use computers to track your productivity and match it against your co-workers. Have they joined the thousands of companies that chart all of your telephone activity—long distance and local—to see who you are calling, how many times you are calling the number, and how long you are talking on the phone each time? Have they weighed you down with cell phones, beepers, and PDAs that keep you connected to the office, regardless of where you are? Some workplace security systems are so sophisticated that your employer knows where you are in the building at any time. You think you are being spied on? Well, you are. That's life in a century when technology is sold as the means to maximum productivity. Never mind the fact that it is making us so uncomfortable that we can't relax in our jobs and do our best work. This is just reality, something we have to learn to live with because, for the moment, we have no choice.

Some people have used that environment to their advantage. I just read an article about an employee who installed a program on his Palm Pilot that let him remotely change the documents that appeared on the screen of his office desktop, no matter where he was. He could have been on the golf course or at a Starbuck's. If his boss strolled by, the changing documents on his screen made it appear that he'd just stepped away for a moment. Some people have rigged things so they can send documents to the office printer when they aren't even in the building. Timers in e-mail programs can send notes for when you're out shopping or sunning on the beach.

If I were signing the paychecks of those people, I'd be outraged. As someone who sees the intrusion of all this technology, I think it is pretty funny—and the natural result of what happens when Big Brother disempowers Little Brother. I completely understand the need to take power back when you feel power has been taken from you. That is the essence of that age-old tradition of taking a "mental health day," calling in sick, even though you don't have a fever. You aren't sick. You are just sick of *them*. As a manager, I understood the value of employees doing that every now and again. I just hoped they had a good time and remembered to wear sunscreen so they didn't come back with a great tan.

How can you comfortably work in an environment where you know you are being watched? Try to ascertain what is really going on. Don't let the grapevine distort the extent of the spying. There may be certain occasions where it is safe to ask about what your employer is doing to keep tabs on you. For example, if your boss has a brown-bag lunch session, you can ask if it is safe to send an occasional personal e-mail or make a personal call, if necessary. If the grapevine is swirling with talk about the latest spy software that has been put on your computers, why not say, "Hey, there are a lot of rumors that our computers have little men inside them that are watching what we are doing. What's the truth?" Once you know what is being done, you then need to see how the information is being used. They can say they read e-mails, but if they never do anything about it, it's not the threat you might assume. If somebody gets scolded, put on probation, or fired for making personal calls, you know you'd better not do it.

I know that some offices expect 100 percent professionalism 100 percent of the time. How can people function when they are so restricted? Does the increase in productivity make up for the slide in morale that inevitably comes when people feel they aren't valued as human beings?

Do you have any choice but to learn to live with these new invasions? Well, you can change work environments, or you can make peace with the one you are in. I always figured, if somebody had time to read all of my e-mails, then they could make a go at it. I'm not going to be afraid to breathe.

When Should I Worry?

Mustangs can be pretty high maintenance. Sometimes, it comes with the turf. Rocking that ol' boat doesn't endear you to certain people—no matter how right you are. Speaking up on issues like diversity and gender equality made me some very fierce enemies who were bent on foiling my career. What I learned from that is you shouldn't stand out front if you aren't willing to get shot at. If you take the mustang path, there will be moments when it really *is* all about you.

That makes it especially important to know how to tell when you should worry and when you shouldn't. Rather than focus entirely on how another person reacts to you, look hard at how he or she reacts to others. When you know that person is under pressure for some external reason, does he or she carry that anxiety into situations with you? If it's not all about you, what might it really be about?

> 'I've learned that everything I think I am seeing isn't real. There is always more than meets the eye."
>
> —BRETT BUTLER, actress and comedian

Before you allow yourself to feel slighted, insulted, or hurt, take some time to shift perspectives. What is really going on with that person?

My friend called her boss at her part-time job to see if she could change her schedule. He seemed distant and annoyed. She got off the phone and said, "I'm afraid I stressed him out." The guy's wife was having their baby any minute. I doubt he cared one bit about her needing to in the future. "It's not all about you," I said. "Yes it is," she joked.

Just chill! What you worry about today will probably be forgotten in a couple of weeks. Why let your mind play games and make matters much worse? Listen to Sally Priesand, the first woman ordained as a rabbi in this country. "I have my worry rule," she said. "If you need to worry, sit down for 15 minutes and really worry. Then say, 'Okay. I did my worrying for today. Now let's get on with it.' "

A MOMENT OF
ACCEPTANCE
WITH
Esmeralda Santiago

Author Esmeralda Santiago braved rejection and culture clashes from the time she moved to the United States until she channeled her feelings and experiences into her writing. She is the author of two popular memoirs, When I Was Puerto Rican *and* Almost a Woman, *and a novel,* America's Dream.

The first defining moment in my life was at 13, when I came to the United States, not speaking a word of English. My parents weren't getting along, and I thought it was a temporary move. We moved from a barrio with no electricity in a rural part of Puerto Rico to the center of Brooklyn. I was the eldest in a family of seven children that eventually became a family of 11 children managed by a single mother. Not only had my father abandoned us, but he wanted no part in our life in the United States.

There was no bilingual education. They just dumped you into a class with slow learners, and their assumption was that if you didn't know English, you weren't very smart. I knew I wasn't one of the dumb kids, so I went about teaching myself English, going to the library to get a children's illustrated alphabet book. At first, I learned all the nouns from the picture books. Then the adjectives. I eventually began to get the rest of the sentences by reading more advanced children's books. No one was guiding me in this, but the year after I arrived, I was reading on a tenth grade level.

I didn't go back to Puerto Rico until 12 years after we'd arrived in the United States. That was the second big defining moment in my life. I'd accomplished so many things that would be hard for anyone—not just a poor Puerto Rican girl. But, going back was devastating. I was 25, I'd learned English, I'd been a working person in New York City, never depending on welfare or any charity. I'd graduated from Harvard magna cum laude on scholarship and did all the things I thought people should congratulate me on.

All they said was, "You aren't really Puerto Rican. You're so Americanized. You are too aggressive to be a Puerto Rican woman." I didn't dress the way a Puerto Rican woman should dress. I had an accent.

Who set up those rules? Who said, if you speak English really well, you are less Puerto Rican than others? Who said, if you are aggressive, you are less Puerto Rican? I didn't feel like a different person. I felt like a Puerto Rican country girl who had moved to the city and made her own life without being dependent on others.

I didn't belong anywhere.

In the United States, I was Puerto Rican. In Puerto Rico, I was American. I'd hoped to use my experience and education to do good things in Puerto Rico, but when I tried to find a job, the best I could get was as a receptionist. And I had a Harvard degree! I came back to the United States, but when I returned, I was suicidal. There was an incredible sense of aloneness and powerlessness.

Within six months, I met the man I am married to. My life began again. It was a very big thing getting to the point where I said, "I don't care what they think about me. I could not be any better person than I am." That was freeing, because it was no longer about trying to please other people. It was about trying to please myself.

I got a job working for an agency that served Puerto Ricans in the Boston area. There were no services for them. Having been through the experiences they were all undergoing, it was a great opportunity to use what I'd learned in college, and on my jobs, but to also use my compassion and knowledge of that population to do something to improve their lives. Friends said, "You're going back to the ghetto." I said, "I'll just see if I can make a difference." It was very moving to me to design a program, write proposals, and raise money to help people like the one I once was. It was so satisfying to give something back.

I felt like all the struggles and suffering I had gone through were useful to me and helpful to other people who were facing the same challenges. I need to express myself. I love to sing, but I can't. I was a dancer for many years, but my body decided I couldn't dance anymore. I loved to draw, but couldn't draw well. I was a devoted reader. Through the reading, I was training myself to be a writer. I began to write. I wrote about issues I did not see anywhere else. I felt completely alone, but I figured there must be other people feeling what I was feeling. I would write for them.

After I became a writer, I went back to Puerto Rico. I was celebrated! I'm very well-known there now. My books are read in the schools, and at the universities. People are writing dissertations about them and conferences are given about them. I've become a celebrity in a way I never imagined. I'm respected as a literary figure.

So, this is why I am here. We all wonder at one time why we were born, why we are here. A lot of people never find the answer. I'm lucky.

JUST GET IT DONE

Daring to Make Mistakes

SHE'D had it. For months, Claudia Kennedy had been reminded weekly that her battalion of more than 200 intelligence officers and soldiers had not trained at the shooting range. There was always some problem—the buses didn't show up, there weren't time slots open at the range, there were problems arranging replacements so everybody on the 24-hour watch could participate. It went on for months, and when her battalion's turn came again, finally "everything looked perfect," said the now-retired, three-star U.S. Army general. "The buses came, the replacement soldiers and officers came, so everybody from all of the shifts on our 24-hour watch could participate and the more than 200 people who needed to fire their guns at the range were ready to board the bus."

Not so fast. An officer rushed to Kennedy, who was a lieutenant colonel at the time, and told her someone had mistaken the battalion's basic load of ammunition, which is reserved exclusively for combat, for the training ammo. The training would have to be stopped.

"Take that ammunition and fire it. Go get this training done," Kennedy said.

"I'd had it. It was a huge logistical undertaking. We'd had too many false starts and I figured, enough is enough." Off the battalion went the train. She knew she could have told the brigade commander about the problem in advance and let him decide, but she didn't want her 200 soldiers and intelligence officers to lose another day. "I felt the mechanics of dealing with my scheduling were far more important than dealing with the problem of whether this particular shrink-wrapped load of ammunition was our basic ammunition or not. I didn't figure the Soviets were coming after us anytime soon, and if they were and everything depended on whether my battalion had its basic load, we were in a worse position than I'd thought!"

When the training was over, she called her superior and said, "Colonel Jones, there is good news and bad news in what we've done today. The good news is that we're all trained. The bad news is, we've just fired the basic load." Silence. Then, the colonel let out a low whistle. He said, "Claudia, Claudia . . ." "After that, the brigade commander worked me over pretty hard on it," she said. She doesn't remember if she got a letter of reprimand or not. But, it was a *huge* deal in the moment, and a nothing deal in her career.

"Oh, it was considered a *huge* mistake," Kennedy said. "About every two years, there would be something, some kind of a mistake, but in the long run, they didn't matter." Kennedy went on to become the first woman to become a three-star general in the U.S. Army. Some mistakes seem like they are the end of the world, but they are not, she said. They just aren't.

Stop being chicken! Sometimes, you have to take the risks you need to take in order to get the job done. There is seldom the perfect moment to make the perfect decision, so stop waiting. There comes a time when you have to stop tiptoeing and start stomping your feet. Just figure out what you need to do, then do it. The "act now, get permission later" movement has gained a lot of momentum, and for good reason. Things tend to work out. You will make a few bad calls in life, but at least you are making calls, intent on moving forward. If you wait to deal with every possible obstacle, you'll never do anything.

Along the way, you'll make mistakes. AT&T president Betsy Bernard sure does. "I make 'em every day, but it's a lot like skiing. To get better, you have to wipe out. If you don't, you are never going to get better, and you are not pushing yourself. You have to break down to break through. You can call that making mistakes, but it is necessary for continuous improvement." Again and again, power women have told me the most critical element for success is the ability to take a risk. So many of us fear risk because we fear failing, but if we have vision and truly want to get things done, we really don't have time to waste on some astrological confluence when everything comes together and we know for certain that everything is going to work out okay. Sometimes, you've got to fire that basic load of ammunition and hope for the best. Stop whining and just get it done.

Get Out of Your Own Way

It's easy to talk yourself out of anything, so stop talking. Nobody wants to fail—*nobody*. But, you will never succeed if you can't risk failing, and if you aren't failing a little, you aren't testing your limits. It is that simple. How has failure affected your life? Hasn't every failure made you grow up in some way? But, fear of failing is just one of many reasons you can hold yourself back.

Are you afraid of succeeding? Plenty of us are. You're a grown woman, and you can handle your success because you do deserve it. If you are worried that you still won't be happy if and when you achieve your goal, get over it. You're living all wrong if you are waiting to be happy after you have achieved something. You could die tomorrow, so be happy now. Enjoy the thrill of trying something new and persevering toward your success.

Some people hold themselves back because they fear they will be embarrassed by success and intimidated by the accolades they might get. Well, there aren't going to be any accolades if you do nothing, and if you do achieve your goal, you should enjoy what you have done. Why not celebrate your growth so others know they can do it, too?

Some people fear that achieving their goal will only lead to tougher expectations for the next challenge. Well, get over that, too. You'll do what you want to do in this life, when you want to do it. As long as you are chasing your own dreams and goals, you'll be much happier than you will if you keep trying to figure out how to please the rest of the world. Applause on the outside is kind of nice. When it comes from within, it is absolutely beautiful. Live your way.

Maybe you fear you'll lose your spark, energy, or momentum once you accomplish what you have set out to do. Get over that, too. You are in charge of finding that spark. If being the CEO isn't a thrill anymore, go take a pottery class. You'll find your spark where you want to find it.

It's amazing how many people don't try things because they keep playing out a bunch of crazy "what if" scenarios that make it seem like they have no control over their lives. Ultimately, you have control over the most important part of living: how you choose to feel about life right in this very moment. That's what gives you the power to take chances! If you look at it as a pass-fail, win-lose situation, you can talk yourself out of anything. If you look at it as more material in your life's story—an adventure that will teach you something new—then it's not quite so daunting. You only get one chance to live your life, so why choose the boring path, and why be too chicken to cross that path because you are afraid of what is on the other side? The other side is where all the excitement is.

Getting it done often comes down to discipline, a word I never liked because it seemed like it would turn my creative process into some sort of regiment. I was never all that disciplined, but when I quit my job to work at home as a writer, I knew I had to discipline myself. Suddenly, I was in charge of my destiny, and my time management, planning, and work habits would impact my future directly. What I did would no longer help or hurt the company. It would help or hurt me. You can't use a lack of discipline as an excuse for not doing something. It's a lack of will. A lot of idea people don't like the process of writing down lists, schedules, goals, and objectives. But, deal with it. It doesn't take much time to come up with the framework of a plan, and once you have it, all you have to do is leap.

Take Charge of Your World

Suspense novel superstar Mary Higgins Clark said she's always been put off by wannabe writers who say they are going to write a book as soon as the children are grown or as soon as they switch jobs. She says "as soon as" are three fatal words that keep us mired in excuses. If you want to do it, just do it. "I love to write," she said. "I'd write if no one else even read it. To thine own self be true."

If anyone ever had an excuse to put her dream on hold, it was Clark. She was 35 years old when her husband died of heart failure, leaving her to raise their five children. Despite the demands of working—writing radio scripts and taking care of her children—Clark was so driven to write fiction that she'd get up every day at 5 a.m. and spend two hours weaving the stories that would eventually propel her into the stratosphere and onto the bestseller lists as an internationally renowned suspense writer. It paid off. Her latest four-book contract with Simon and Schuster was for $64 million.

But, it took a "get it done" attitude. Yes, she worked hard for her children, but she didn't lose herself to the stress. She cherished what she had. "You feel overwhelmed when you have a bunch of little kids in the house, but it goes so quickly. They are growing up and growing up more. Don't lose those wonderful years because you are in a tough situation. Anyone who has put aside their motherhood, leaving them to nannies— they are crazy. I had to work, many women have to work, but when you get home, be there. I was home, I wasn't out. You have to be. You *must* be. Kids understand the difference between your being away from them because it is necessary or your being away from them because you damn well choose to be away from them. Never underestimate a two year old."

The joy of family transcended anything her writing success could have given her, she said. "Now that the books have worked and been successful, I am still the same person. The most important thing is the home and the family. The celebrity part is something else way over there because it will come and it will go. The people who take it too seriously are very, very foolish. When the chips are down, it's your family and friends that count.

Listen to Your Gut

"We have this God-given gift of a women's intuition, but we don't use it," said Geraldine Laybourne, founder, chairman, and CEO of the Oxygen network. "Eighty percent of all business decisions are made on intuition and 20 percent on analysis. I always tried to make decisions based on what is for the greater good. The only time I have ever felt good about anything was if I felt good about it. It's when you know it is good. You don't need some goofy CEO to tell you that it is good."

Listen to your gut. That's what Laybourne did when she decided to listen to what children said they wanted on television, rather than what all the conventional experts said was needed. In the 1980s, she turned an infant cable network into what is our beloved Nickelodeon—that $8 billion mega network for kids. Laybourne left Nickelodeon for Disney/ABC Cable Networks and supervised the company's interest in everything from Lifetime to E!, A&E, and The Disney Channel. From there, she thought it was time to build a power network for women. In 1998, Oxygen was born.

When she's out there on the limb and a project she's involved with is having problems, Laybourne doesn't give up. She and I talked as Oxygen was in its third year and still having trouble taking off. She said she kept telling herself, "It's just a matter of time. We are a complete and utter rare commodity. It is impossible for me to think we won't make it. Everyone has this idea that it was easy to do Nickelodeon. It took seven years to get a hit." She didn't whine; she just did what she had to do.

Laybourne remembers building a fort in her back yard at age ten. Her dad came out and told her to come in. It was dark. "Dad said, 'It is good enough.' I said, 'Dad, I want it to be better.' He said, 'Look out world.' It is that stubborn streak that got me here."

The only way to get beyond your fears and get things done is to just put your fears aside and move forward. Some of that comes natural to Laybourne. She was the second child, sandwiched between one sister who was perfect and beautiful, and the other who was brilliant and charismatic, she said. Her dad looked at her and said, "You are going to be my business daughter." She was. "He was a stockbroker and a real gambler. I got a little bit infected by that kind of risk taking and it influenced what I did with my career." Laybourne's father would take her to business meetings and give her proformas for companies. At age eight, she was making investment recommendations. "He never took my advice," she said. "He always went for the Tidy Toilets instead of Disney." Her mother hammered into her the need to do something good in the world and be financially independent, and her dad passed on his enormous confidence in her.

With that confidence, she went to college and became a teacher. She remembers walking down the aisle with her husband, also a teacher, and laughing "that we were the most downwardly mobile couple in America. We had no intention of making money. We had every intention of doing something with kids and creativity." So, did it have to be in the classroom? A few years later, as program manager for the fledgling network Nickelodeon, she was able to focus on "giving kids something better than the dreck they were getting on television."

"I didn't care about a corner office. I cared about creating a franchise for kids that could never be taken away from them. So when bad business decisions were put in front of me that I thought threatened that, I could never go that way, even though it might be good for the bottom line for that quarter. I was mission driven." By being driven by this sense of mission, she ultimately became vice president.

Of course it is exactly that drive and dedication to mission that led her up that ladder, long ago putting her high on the list of the most powerful women in America. So what could have possibly induced her to leave that stability and success to start Oxygen? How could she? Her power and position were so secure. "People ask how I had the guts to start Oxygen," she said. "If you could own—well, I don't own it completely, but I have a large ownership stake in a media company—and if you could do that and it would be the first time a woman has had the chance to own a television network, you would do that. That doesn't seem like a risk. The big risk was leaving Nickelodeon. It was my personality, it was my humor, it was my team, it was my baby. It's amazing that I did it. What was scary to me at Nickelodeon was that I had taken risk after risk for kids and Nickelodeon, and I had not ever taken a risk for myself. What was scary was that I was getting lazy, that I was feeling complacent, and that terrified me. I felt like I needed to throw myself out the window and shake myself up, which I indeed did."

It's amazing how some women so boldly leave their ruts, and some won't. Every time I give a speech, I meet at least a half-dozen women who tell me they know they need to make changes in their lives, but they just can't make the move. They're worried about failing. And money. They're worried about insecurity and uncertainty. They figure they'll do something someday, but have no idea when that someday is or how they will make changes. It shakes me up to hear the desperation in their voices, and I wish I could give them the magic answers they think I have that will solve everything. I can't tell you what to do or how to do it. I can coach a plan out of you, work out a calendar, and ride you until you get something done. But in the end, if you want to do something, do it. You want success? Go get it. Just make up your mind. Break big challenges into small steps. Attach a calendar, assigning deadlines to those steps, and just get busy.

If you give yourself an inch to fail, you'll fail. I truly believe that. The greatest success stories have been manifestations of great vision and drive from people who would not give themselves that inch to fail. I was talking about that with singer Joan Armatrading, whose mighty voice, deeply felt lyrics, and stunning stage presence have made her an international star for more than 30 years. "I know a chap in England that I thought was one of the best musicians and songwriters and singers. You'd think he'd have everything going for him," Armatrading said. "For some reason, he couldn't make it happen. So it's talent, it's perseverance, and it's luck."

But, you have to see and believe in the possibility in order for it to manifest. You can't control the elements or the obstacles, but the one thing you must control is your focus and drive. Again, if you give yourself an inch to fail, you will fail.

"I'm one of those people who thinks if you want something enough—really enough—and you know that you're going to work for it, in a lot of cases it's going to happen," Armatrading said. "If you have a very strong belief, you can make it work. I'm the sort of person if there's something that I really want to do, I'll just go and do it. If I don't succeed in something, I'll come back to it." That is what Armatrading did when it came time to go back to get her college degree. She just went back and did it. Her songwriting talent is extraordinary, yet that skill came naturally to her. School was different. "The degree was a very big learning process for me," she said. "I had to learn how they wanted me

Your "Get It Done" Plan

The next time you face a major challenge, start by assigning yourself a morning to come up with your "get it done" strategy. It's amazing how much time you will save by taking time to breathe and figure out how you can best implement your plan.

On a big piece of paper, write down every possible step you know you need to take in order to make your vision live. Just brainstorm and write everything down in no particular order.

Now sort them into four categories:

1. Beginning
2. Ongoing
3. Middle
4. End

Rank the beginning and ongoing items in importance, and note how often you will need to take action on those matters. As you progress through this plan, you can rank the middle and end categories, but those will change as you discover how things are really played out.

Type everything up, and on the top of the page, write something inspirational that will keep you moving forward. Personally, I like the line, "Shut up and do the work." Make a note of the places where you expect to encounter difficulties, and mark "reward moments" right after those obstacles are dealt with. Then, you can schedule a massage or a night out around your successes.

Get input on your plan from your close friends and mentors. Check in with them regularly for support.

You know what you have to do, so do it.

to write everything—the amount of words, the language to use, how to reference and quote things, and obviously, learning the different topics. That was an effort and a real process. It was quite startling to know that I knew so little when I started." She didn't whine. She just made up her mind to get that history degree and got it done. "There was no question that I'd get that degree with honors," Armatrading declared. When she got the diploma, she was "over the moon." "When it really hit home was when I had my graduation ceremony and I was with all the other students. I felt like an achiever. I was so nervous waiting to go on stage and get the paper. When I got the diploma, the applause for me was really good because it was like saying, 'You're an artist, but you've taken time to do what we're doing.' "

I contrast her story with those of several stunningly successful women in business who have admitted to me that they are ashamed of themselves because they don't have their college degrees. They completely overlook or dismiss what they have accomplished and focus on how they fall short because they lack a diploma, which they see as some sort of pedigree. I met a senior vice president of a major bank who was terrified of speaking to a college business class because she felt inferior to juniors and seniors in college! She had a nationally prominent position in business and could easily have written their textbooks, yet she didn't have the piece of paper that, to her, validated her expertise. "If it bugs you so bad, why don't you just go back to school?" I asked. She shrugged. I have the feeling she was afraid she wouldn't cut it.

Success starts with your idea and your total commitment on all levels—personal, political, and perhaps economic. There is the time commitment, too. Move forward with the absolute solid, unflinching certainty that what you are doing is the right thing for you to be doing. If you can talk yourself out of doing something, or out of doing it now, you probably don't want it that badly. If you want it, go make it happen.

Act Your Truth

I love the stories of trailblazer Marie Wilson, former president of the Ms. Foundation for women for two decades. She's learned to punt, be clever, play the game, and fight for what she wants. In the process, she's raised millions of dollars for programs that support women and girls. In fact, Take Our Daughters to Work Day was her brainchild. "I had a great mentor," she said. "He was a man, and years ago he told me, 'You don't have to conform, Marie. You just have to look like it.' He had a crew cut, but he was the most radical man I have ever met. Until the world changes and it is safer to be a strong, shitkicking woman, we need to figure out how to understand the culture and move in a way we can get things done." Exactly. When she started working for the Ms. Foundation, the organization had very little money in the bank. "On the first day, I bought clothes. I started walking around, talking like we were doing great. I never went around saying, 'We are poor, you need to help these poor women.' It's like, 'We're doing great!' One of my friends grabbed me and said, 'You can't even pay next month's rent!' I said, 'You keep quiet about that.' You have to give people a vision about what can happen, and you have to act as if it can happen and you have to believe it can happen. It's acting into the truth."

You define that truth. There will be others who will try to distract or derail you, but your biggest obstacle—or asset—is you. It's your choice. If you get discouraged, waste time whining, and give yourself an out so you don't have to keep pushing, you can turn a great vision into a pile of self-doubt. If you remain determined, focused, and sure you will succeed, you're on your way. See your vision, then give it life.

Move Forward Rather Than Standing Still

It is all a learning process, and if you find yourself on the mustang path, there will be many moments when you aren't quite sure where to go, but you will be sure that you must go somewhere. One woman who knows all about that is Mavis Leno, who helped drive the cause of the Afghanistan women repressed by the Taliban onto the front page. Leno is chair of the Feminist Majority Foundation's Campaign to Stop Gender Apartheid in Afghanistan, and has been our nation's most visible and blunt critic of the Taliban's treatment of women. She is also Jay Leno's wife.

As a member of the board of the Feminist Majority—one of the nation's premier organizations fighting for equality—she was privy to updates on what the Taliban was doing to oppress Afghan women long before 9-11. Before the Taliban rule spread in the mid-1990s, women comprised 60 percent of the Afghan population and had equal rights. Women wore what they wanted, moved freely through society, and had jobs at every level. When the Taliban came to power, the women were ordered home, banned from working in any capacity, and punished if they left home without being completely covered by a burqua and accompanied by a close male relative. They could not gather with more than one unrelated woman at a time. Education was forbidden. Medical care was almost nonexistent.

In 1997, the Taliban ran two-thirds of Afghanistan. Leno, a strong feminist, wanted to do something about it, but what? She had to learn to find her power and her voice. "The news media didn't want to cover it, but overnight, after the Taliban came in, it was like the women were buried alive," Leno said. "The Taliban took away their computers and their satellite televisions because they didn't want any information going out or coming in. These women didn't know if anyone knew what happened to them. There had been no outcry." The issue grabbed her. She knew her last name could help her get visibility for the issue, so she volunteered to help. They needed press coverage, but didn't get it. "I spent a lot of time feeling like I was scaling a stone wall," she said.

The biggest stone wall was a shareholder's meeting for Unical, which was planning to build an oil pipeline across Afghanistan. "I got up and asked how they could contemplate essentially financing a terrible regime like the Taliban. I said, 'You are an American company with all the rights and privileges that conveys, and the least you can do is uphold American principles wherever you take your business. You can't passively and fiscally support monsters like the Taliban.' I was very nervous." Despite coming to the meeting with all her facts and figures, Leno felt patronized by the man who ran the shareholder's meeting. "I went out feeling like that was a completely useless thing I had done, but it was the first shot in what was obviously going to be a long battle. To my amazement, about six months later, Unical announced they were not going to further pursue putting a gas pipeline through Afghanistan. They had a number of reasons, but they also cited the Feminist Majority for making them aware of what the Taliban regime was doing that was so oppressive to women. That was the first time I realized how little it takes sometimes to make an impact in a situation."

That is why it is so important to keep marching forward. You may think you need to do x, y, and z—in that order—to accomplish your goal, but sometimes there is one element of your plan, something you thought wouldn't matter, that winds up being most important. "The first few things I did for this cause left me completely terrified. When I came home, I waited for the remorse to roll over me, but it didn't. This was something very deep inside of me, so deep that I didn't even know it was there. I was waiting to do something like this."

Despite her efforts, she and the Feminist Majority still couldn't get press coverage for the issue. She tried to be strategic. "I wanted to be a warrior for these women and go out and fight a great battle for them. That means going out with all the weapons you have in your arsenal. My husband's success is a big weapon. It's not like he ever put anything in the monologue for me. He had me on the show a couple of times and I got to mention briefly what was going on, but it's an entertainment show and a lot of people with good causes want to get on. He didn't want to be perceived as making an exception for me." Still, he was extremely supportive. Leno said her husband had very high expectations of her "in the best sense." Sometimes he has more faith in her than she has in herself, she said.

The very first year the Taliban was in power, Leno said, she floundered, trying to get attention to the issue. "Then I had this great revelation. I had been completely concentrating on what I didn't know and focusing on my fear of not being a good enough warrior for these women." It came to her that she didn't know how to deal with the "serious" press on an issue, but she sure as heck knew how to get things into the popular media. Her dad was an actor. Most of the people she knew were involved in the entertainment business on some level. She told Jay that they were going to hold press conferences in New York and Los Angeles to announce a $100,000 donation from them to the campaign to fight gender apartheid in Afghanistan. Instead of begging the *New York Times* for coverage, she basked in coverage from magazines like *People* and *Us* as well as from radio shows, magazines, and newspapers that covered celebrity and entertainment happenings. The "serious" media may have missed how riveting the story was, but working Americans got it as soon as it hit the popular press. Brilliant. "This cause did not go from the top echelon, from the most educated people on down," said Leno. "It went from the grassroots up! It was real people saying, 'Not on our watch. This is not going to happen.' "

Remember the petitions that circulated via e-mail? They circulated and recirculated worldwide, calling on humans everywhere to agree. The petitions said, "In signing this, we agree that the current treatment of women in Afghanistan is completely *unacceptable* and deserves action by the United Nations and that the current situation overseas will not be tolerated." I got that petition so many times I wondered how it could even matter if I signed it. There was certainly nothing scientific or accurate about the way the signatures were being collected. But, they did matter in a huge way. "It is incredible how little action you have to take to make a difference," Leno said. "All those petitions that women signed gave us so much access with the State Department because they were literally drowning in those petitions. This was back during the Clinton administration. They told us they got more phone calls and letters on this issue than any other. That was just, mainly, women sitting down and signing that petition and sending it in. "The will of the people has a huge impact. If your constituents are writing tons of letters, well, television network executives assume one letter represents a thousand people who felt the same but didn't write." Rally your troops. Take your ammunition and fire it.

Blowing the Whistle

Some mustangs find themselves in a position when they know they have to fire their ammunition, they know it's going to create a real blast, and they know they have to do it alone. When you need courage, remember the story of Sherron Watkins, the Enron vice president who blew the whistle on accounting irregularities that made her "incredibly nervous that we will implode in a wave of accounting scandals." She knew she was right, and went to Enron CEO Ken Lay, who she felt certain was as a man of integrity who would hear the message and not shoot the messenger. Instead, he and the old boys closed ranks and tried to force Watkins out and mute her story. As the financial press pieced together the mess at Enron, the company's board of directors commissioned a report that proved Watkins right: the company's executives had gained millions from side deals and partnerships that violated accounting rules and ethics. Their dealings led to the bankruptcy of Enron, and the pensions of lifelong employees and investors were drained, even though the top executives had walked away with the riches before facing prosecutors.

"I have seen the life of a vindicated whistleblower, but it was compacted into a time span of six months," said Watkins, who was named person of the year for 2002 along with whistleblowers Coleen Rowley of the FBI and Cynthia Cooper at WorldCom. "You do this because you think your company is going to listen to you and you are going to effect change. Then you realized that's not true. You are treated like a pariah, shoved down to a low-level floor to an office with old furniture and not much to do. You start to become a conspiracy nut. I kept wondering, 'Have all those people who I thought were ethical gone over to the dark side?' It really is a bleak feeling when you think everyone is against you and you are swimming upstream by yourself."

There will be times when you have to swim in the other direction alone. It's scary and lonely. That's why, when you see another woman swimming alone, you should give support in every way possible. Watkins remembered how much those "You go girl!" and "You're my hero" e-mails meant to her. "The tiniest words of encouragement are helpful," she said.

Some would-be whistleblowers approach Watkins after she speaks to ask her what they should do. She tells them to be very, very careful. "First of all, a lot of whistleblowers get fired. That shuts them up in a hurry because they have to find a job. And, they can't complain too much about their former employer when they are trying to figure out how to pay their own mortgages." Still, sometimes, there is no other choice. "At the end of your life, you have to know you stood for what is right," she said. "Your only choice is to tell the truth."

A MOMENT OF
RESOLVE
WITH
Tracie Cone

Tracie Cone and her domestic partner, Anna Marie dos Remedios, left major-league newspaper jobs to take over their hometown weekly. Overnight, they turned the advertising "shopper" paper into a journalistic pit bull that so unraveled one town leader that he got even electronically. It took a painful federal hate crimes lawsuit to unmask the four-term city councilman. The story made international headlines, but, more than anything, it defined a conservative small town for its character. The Pinnacle, *which had never previously won a journalism award, has become California's most award-winning paper in the California Newspaper Publisher's Association contest. Both Cone and dos Remedios were named California Newspaper Executives of the Year.*

I was never taken seriously as a management type in the newsroom. Maybe that's my own fault. I've been funny, crazy, and, early on, it might have been my sexual orientation. In the back of my head, I thought, "I'm always going to be a reporter. A 65-year-old reporter."

Anna and I bought a five-acre ranch in San Benito County in a rural area way off the beaten path. It was isolated, very small, and ranching and farming were still the number-one industries. I'd never lived in a community that was not served by good journalism, and neither of the local newspapers called growth into question or challenged the hold developers had on city hall. San Benito County was the fastest-growing county in California.

There were two papers: a weekly and a really crappy five-day-a-week paper. The shopper was owned by a family-owned grocery store that was being sold to Safeway. I said to Anna, "Hey, I bet since they are selling the grocery store, they won't want the shopper." One meeting led to another meeting and to another. It's like dating someone you don't really like. After you've gone out three times, you feel like you have led them on and you have to figure some graceful way of getting out of it. I never could, and we bought the paper. We knew nothing about running a business or putting out a paper, but we quit union-protected newspaper jobs with five weeks paid vacation to step into a job where we were working 18 hours a day, seven days a week with no vacations.

We started doing stories questioning the good-old-boy network and the developers, and wrote editorials advocating that we dramatically slow down growth. When a growth moratorium was lifted, the council immediately gave out every permit to an out-of-town developer. The developer would build homes for people in San Jose who wanted to move to the country and pay $450,000 for homes in a community where the average household income is $30,000 a year. It was all growth for people who didn't live here.

I wrote an editorial calling the decision moronic. At a public hearing, the locals begged them not to approve it. I had a photographer there, and every time she pointed her camera at the council member who was the ringleader of all this, he would put up his middle finger at the side of his face, obviously flipping her off, we think, so we couldn't use a photo of him. I thought, "That doesn't ruin it. That just shows who he is." So, we ran a picture of someone testifying in the foreground and Councilman Joe Felice flipping off our photographer. We were deluged with letters and phone calls. Everyone was so angry with him.

A couple weeks later, I opened an e-mail that linked me to what looked like a parody of the *Pinnacle*. I thought we'd been spoofed, which was great, but the first thing I saw was my name on a hyperlink that said, "Tracie Cone chats with her girlfriends." I clicked on it, and it went to a hard-core lesbian pornography site. It also had our columnist's photo over a column that had him "confessing" to being a convicted child molester in the 1960s while he was under the influence of drugs. None of it was true. When I looked at the counter on the site, I noticed I was visitor 947. My first reaction was that it was Joe Felice. I called the city manager and said, "I don't know what is going on, but it is frightening and you'd better hope it is not Joe Felice." He said, "Everybody at City Hall has seen it."

It took 30 days to get Yahoo to shut it down, but it kept popping up elsewhere. We filed a federal lawsuit alleging civil rights crimes, copyright violations, and defamation, and tried to get a subpoena that would help us find out who did it. The lawsuit was big news. We had to write about it.

There we were, in a multigenerational, conservative ranching community where California's Defense of Marriage act passed with 66 percent of the vote. We were just trying to be good journalists, but we were in the position of having to print very personal information about ourselves on the front page. We had to out ourselves. We really thought it would destroy our business because we were afraid people would be frightened of us and wouldn't want to support our newspaper. But, we felt we had to file it. We cried. I take the role we play in this community very seriously. I provide incomes to 20 families. There were people on our own staffs who didn't know we were gay. I had this vision that everything was going to collapse. The story came out on Thursday and I thought, by Friday, there wouldn't be anything left.

I still get choked up when I think about what happened. Everybody in this community thought it was unfair. Old-time ranchers, little old ladies—there were calls and letters and visits. They'd come down here and take off their cowboy hats and say, "We don't care who you are, just that you give us a good newspaper. We admire what you've done." They brought us plates of cookies and stopped us on the streets. It was the opposite of what I thought was going to happen.

When the suit was filed, newspapers latched on to the story of the small-town, crusading journalists trying to do the right thing. Plus, there was the gay element. The *San Francisco Chronicle* wrote the first story, then the *Mercury News,* Associated Press, and all the television stations. From all that publicity came volunteers who wanted to help us. There was this cadre of volunteers in the Silicon Valley who went to work as soon as we got the ISP number and they helped us find out that the account that created the website was registered to Councilman Joe Felice. The *Los Angeles Times* did a front page story. It was in *USA Today.* We plugged our names into Google and there was a story in Arabic!

At first, Felice denied it, but, as it got closer to going to court, his family was demoralized and angry with him and he was devastated. We didn't want to completely destroy the man. All we wanted was for him to admit he did it, and apologize for it. We settled for $50,000 and a written apology. We gave the money to charities in our community in $10,000 increments, and, we gave to the National Center for Lesbian Rights because we wanted him to know his money went to fight injustices to gay people.

The point I always want to make about this is that we always tried to do the right thing. We were honest, and we didn't back away from what we had to do journalistically, even though we thought it would kill us. The moral is that if you are true to your principles and stay true—no matter how difficult it might be—everything seems to work out.

12.

BACK AT THE RANCH

Uniting with Other Mustangs

"THE women's movement was a failure!" a 21 year old proclaimed in her speech to a group of professional women attending an annual conference. She was competing for an award as a future business leader, and concluded that the movement failed because women still aren't getting equal pay. If I'd had a tomato, I'd have thrown it right at her.

I waited a couple of hours before I stopped her for a little chat.

It's wasn't that she didn't appreciate what the women before her had done for her, it was that she had no clue about it. "You need to know what the women's movement accomplished," I told her. "Do you realize that it wasn't that long ago that there were two sets of classified ads in the paper—one advertising jobs for men, the other for women?" Her eyes widened. "Or that you couldn't have gotten a credit card unless your husband got it for you in his name? Do you realize that it hasn't been that long since banks wouldn't give mortgages to women, even when they were the prime breadwinners? Not long ago, there weren't any sports programs for women." I ran down my list. "There was nothing prohibiting a man from raping his wife. A woman could lose her job for getting pregnant, or could be excluded from the hiring pool if she said she wanted to have a baby *someday*! There was nothing illegal about a male boss telling a woman she needed to service him sexually if she wanted a promotion."

Going over all of this with that young woman made me feel so lucky to have been born at a time when I could watch all of these changes happen. I want to take a moment in this chapter to remind you of how far we've come, because there is so much to celebrate.

Remembering Our Victories

Linda Gordon, women's history professor at New York University reminds us how far we've come. Before the women's liberation movement came together in the late 1960s:

* Medical and law schools had higher stands for women applicants—and most had 20 percent quotas on female admissions.
* There were two sets of classified ads, and women couldn't apply for the jobs for men and men wouldn't want to apply for the jobs for women.
* Access to birth control was limited, and you generally had to pretend to be married to get birth control pills or a diaphragm.
* And sex? Forget that orgasm. In the 1950s, most sex manuals taught one thing: intercourse. If a woman didn't reach orgasm through penile penetration, then she must be frigid. Never mind the clitoris.
* Victims of domestic violence were asked, "What did you do to provoke it? Did you nag him? Put him down?"
* If a woman was raped by a stranger on the street, she was asked what she was doing alone at that hour or why she wore something that would entice the rapist.
* Career choices were completely limited. Secretarial, teaching, and nursing were considered women's work. If you got a college degree, that did nothing to lift you from the expectation that you would get out of college, then live your destiny as a married housewife. Career, if there was one, was always secondary.
* Women's sports were practically invisible.

"The restrictions that have existed for women for all of our history were shattered during my lifetime," said Gail Collins, editor of the *New York Times'* editorial page and author of *America's Women: 400 Years of Dolls, Drudges, Helpmates, and Heroines.* "Nobody has a baby girl and says, 'Too bad she won't be able to do x, y, or z.' For that to change in my lifetime is such a kick to me." But, why don't we celebrate what we've done? "Some people worry that if we celebrate where we have come that we won't be focused on where we need to go. That is obviously true, but it's crazy if you can't sit back and say, 'Hey, this is neat. This is good.' "

Actually, it is impressive that the young woman who spoke about the failure of the women's movement had, at least, seen the pay inequities. Many twentysomethings think things are just fine as they are. I know I did, and so did Betsy Bernard, the president of AT&T. "I started my career in 1977, truly believing I understood women were discriminated against," she said. "I thought I was part of a new generation, a new world. You know, that was then, this is now, let's get on with it, and what about my life? I got into my mid-30s at AT&T and, all of a sudden, there weren't as many women in the positions I was in. It was striking. I remember trying to get a group of women together for a drink and, God, there were not a lot of us." One of her friends said, "Wake up, you Pollyanna, you! This isn't so equal." That was the moment Bernard realized that discrimination still existed, because it clearly was preventing good women from advancing. "That is what causes me to make sure I reach back and keep the door open for those who follow," Bernard said. "Let's not pretend that the door doesn't need a little assistance for those coming behind us. I have the power and influence to do that, and I'd be really remiss and guilt-ridden if I didn't do that." She hadn't been one to join women's groups because she didn't see why she needed them. But then Bernard looked around and realized maybe she wouldn't need them herself, but her involvement might be helpful to others. "What I discovered was, it was helpful and supportive to me," she explained.

It's time for us to all meet back at the ranch and connect and celebrate.

"To me, feminism is not a label," said Mavis Leno, who led the charge against gender apartheid in Afghanistan. "It is a title I am proud to wear. Many, many women died long before I got here, giving their whole lives over so I could be able to identify myself that way. I feel I owe an unpayable debt to the women who came before me. I have a moral obligation to pay it forward."

Sure, we've got a long way to go, but look at where we were. "We started the last century without the right to vote, for God's sake," said Oxygen network CEO Geraldine Laybourne. "We had to play on every playing field like Linda Ellerbee talks about Fred and Ginger; Ginger Rogers did everything that Fred Astaire did except she did it backwards and in high heels. That's what we have done. We have worked on a playing field that is not our natural playing field." It's tough, but rewarding. "If we shine the light on how great it is to be a woman and how we can change the world, it is just breathtaking," she said.

Of course we have a long way to go. Society doesn't change on our timetable, and as we continue our push for equality, we should do it by celebrating how far we have come. That will rev us up for the next battle.

We've Got Work to Do

"We do make it as hard as possible in our country for women to be the best they can," said New York senator Hillary Rodham Clinton. It's a marathon for women with small children to make it in the workforce. Despite the soaring number of women who have entered the workforce in the past 30 years, the bulk of responsibility for child-rearing still belongs to women. "Women still shoulder most of the burden," Clinton said. "It is an impossible situation for most working women to be in. Especially for the women who don't have jobs where they have a certain amount of control over their schedule. These are women who punch clocks and wait tables and have little flexibility over even unpaid leave. They make this mad dash between what they are supposed to do at home and at work."

Take a good look at the figures in the chart contrasting pay for male and female managers. Women are still not paid equivalent to men. The glass ceiling is real, and the impediments for many women to get equal pay for equal work are still considerable, Clinton said. The General Accounting Office recently reported that women in management are *worse* off than they were five years ago, lagging behind in advancement and compensation. "The wage gap actually increased in 1995 to 2000," Clinton said. "We all hear that women make 74, 75, 76 cents to a man's dollar. I used to say, 'That's a problem we ought to fight, but it's also a

Full-Time Female Managers Earn Less Than Their Male Counterparts

NOTE: Inequality exists in *every* industry, but it *got worse in five industries* between 1995 and 2000.

INDUSTRY	FULL-TIME FEMALE MANAGER EARNINGS FOR EVERY $1 EARNED BY MALE FULL-TIME MANAGERS	
	1995	2000
Communications	$0.86	$0.73
Public administration	$0.80	$0.83
Business and repair services	$0.82	$0.83
Entertainment and recreation services	$0.82	$0.76
Other professional services	$0.88	$0.83
Educational services	$0.86	$0.91
Retail trade	$0.69	$0.65
Finance, insurance, and real estate	$0.76	$0.68
Hospitals and medical services	$0.80	$0.85
Professional medical services	$0.90	$0.88

SOURCE: General Accounting Office Study of Women in Management, April 2002

problem of timing. With all these women in the pipeline—young women getting into the workforce—we'll have enough women choosing to post-pone childbearing. We'll have more women on the same level. This will work itself out.' Unfortunately, it hasn't."

We are still living in a competitive work climate that has made way for women to succeed, but not completely flourish. Catalyst, the premier research organization investigating women's workplace issues, recently reported on women in finance-related industries. Seventy percent of the women reported that promotions were rigged in favor of men, and 60 percent lamented that projects and clients were assigned unfairly. Some 65 percent said that women have to work harder than men to achieve the same results. That pits women against men who control the power, and it pits women against other women who sense the only power available is limited. You versus me, me versus you.

The women's movement didn't fail, but those of us who benefited from its accomplishments haven't done a good job of following up and following through.

"We do need to remember that we are standing on somebody else's back," said Christine Todd Whitman, the former Environmental Protec-tion Agency chief and former New Jersey governor. "It is helpful if we turn around, from time to time, and reach out and just make the oppor-tunity for someone else to succeed. It's not about taking someone who isn't ready for a job and putting her in it just so she can be there. It's about making sure you smooth the path so they see where opportunity lies." Whitman tells people that, when in the position to hire between an equally qualified man and woman, choose the woman. That kind of statement can really rankle the status quo, but Whitman explained, "I would never ask anyone to support a woman who they aren't comfort-able with and who is not qualified," she said, but it is important to help the next woman up. Give to others, give to yourself.

Be Wild, Be Clever, Be Bold

We need to exercise our power when we can. That means voting. It means writing public officials and reminding them that you are voting. It means remembering useful facts about women and their advancement so that you are armed and ready when you encounter people spouting false statistics. The way we rid our society of stereotypes and biases is not through legislation or litigation—although there are times when those things help—but by operating as bold, powerful women in society who expect and push for what we deserve.

And, every now and again, we have to cause a ruckus.

The next time you are back at the ranch commiserating with other mustangs, remember that your collective brainpower can be used to achieve some wild things. There is so much to celebrate when you do things right. So, do it right, raise a little hell, and put on your best guerrilla face. That's right. Meet Frida Kahlo. Well, not really Frida Kahlo, the Mexican painter, who died in 1954, but Frida Kahlo of the notorious Guerrilla Girls, who, under this pseudonym, carries out masked protests. It all started in 1984, when the artist and a friend protested the Museum of Modern Art, which was showing an international survey of painting and sculpture that only featured the work of 17 women among the more than 200 artists on display. Many female artists of prominence were not represented in the show. Marching with placards and fury, the artist and her friend formed a traditional picket line to dissuade people from going inside, but their efforts were completely ineffective. Patrons argued with them, or worse, ignored them entirely.

Kalo & Company knew they needed to be bold and creative to get the art world to pay attention to their cause. They looked at their strengths. They knew art, they knew advertising, and they knew how to be creative and resourceful. "We were trying to figure out how to use advertising techniques to make the art world think," Khalo remembered. They decided to print their messages on posters—anonymously—and blanket the area surrounding the museum with the posters and their protest.

One poster said, "Women in America earn only two-thirds of what men do. Women artists earn only one-third of what men do." Another poster said, "Bus companies are more enlightened than NYC art galleries," then showed that 49 percent of the employees at bus companies were women, while only 16 percent of the artists represented by the 33 major New York galleries were women. You can bet those posters got attention—and media coverage. The posters were clever and first class, professionally designed and printed with a notice that they came from the Guerrilla Girls, the "conscience of the art world." They also bore an address for mailing contributions. "We had a request for a photograph for a story, and we had to come up with an appearance. We decided to appear with gorilla masks. We took a pledge of not revealing who we were and took on pseudonyms of dead women artists who'd been forgotten by history or experienced discrimination in their lives. The art world is such a chummy place. To think we were doing something so secretive was fun, and the thought that every woman artist might be a Guerrilla Girl made it kind of exciting—or frightening. People either loved us or hated us. Everyone was talking about us. We wanted to be girls, but we wanted to be freedom fighters who were a little frightening, so we called ourselves the 'Guerrilla Girls.' "

With the exposure, the donations started coming in and things started to change. "We secretly spoke for every woman, and got them off the hook because we were taking the heat. People would call us cowards because we wouldn't put our names behind what we were saying. Well, nobody thought Batman or Superman or Zorro were cowards. We were masked avengers in that tradition." In some cases, their tactics caused galleries and museums to rethink their records. Some art critics even apologized about their lack of articles about women artists.

"You have to figure out really clever ways to present your issues. Being angry sometimes isn't interesting enough to other people," Kahlo said. "You have to get other people interested in your issues, and if you present your anger in an unforgettable way, it works. Humor is something people identify with, even if they don't identify with the issue. It challenges them more than anger."

One of the big lessons here is that you can make a big splash without a big army or a big budget. Their messages reached millions, but how big was their army? Kahlo said the group has always been much smaller than its presence would indicate. Over the past 20 years, perhaps a hundred women have been involved. Total. Talk about power!

Build your army.

Be Free

Years ago, when I interviewed Araceli Segarra about her climb up Mount Everest, she told me, "Life is easier than we make it out to be. You are up there on Everest with a drum of your stuff and you are happy. You come back home and you have a light you can turn on and off, a tub with water, a bathroom, a machine to clean your clothes. And you worry about your car because you got a scratch. You think about that all day and, oh, you forgot the laundry and you forgot the bread. Some people have a bad day, just for that. Why worry? Look at all the things we have and be happy. I can be happy just sitting on a mountain."

Can you? Don't forget, no matter how complicated things get on the mustang path, you always have the freedom to disengage. You can always take a breather and reconnect with another part of yourself that matters more than whatever mission or job you may have.

Former Texas governor Ann Richards warns against defining yourself by your job, because your job is not you, and you are not your job. "After I got beat in the election (by George W. Bush), people asked me

Mustang Mental Health Day

Take a day to disengage from your routine. No e-mails, voice mails, work calls, faxes, piles of mail, Internet clicks or, best of all, no guilt. You work hard enough for everyone else; this is a day to take the time that is just for you. Breathe.

Don't fill the day with too much activity. It's all about slowing down and enjoying who and where you are in life. Journal. Write down what you have that makes you grateful. Feel good about all you have done.

Take a nap on the couch, go for a walk. Make this day the simplest day you will have all year. Just chill and enjoy, because you've earned it.

Once you see how good it feels, you can start making plans to incorporate real "living" time into your routine. It's amazing how easy it is to get lost in the stress you create for yourself. Perhaps you should consider letting some of it go.

how I felt and I would say, 'I mourned two or three seconds, then knew it gave me opportunities to do a lot of things I'd never gotten to do.' The adjustment was so rapid because being governor was my job, but it is not who I am. Once you start confusing yourself with your title, you are in real trouble because you lose sight of what life is all about."

Richards said she will always be known as the former governor of Texas, but that has nothing to do with who she is. "I suppose the thing I value most is my freedom. I work like a dog, but I am free to go and do anything I want to do. I'm not constrained by possessions or need. I have freed myself, I think, to be whoever I want to be. That allows me such an enormous wealth of opportunity. I couldn't even begin to make the list. I don't own anything I have to feed or water, so I can walk out of my apartment here in New York or in Austin and be gone two minutes or 20 years and it won't matter. I encourage women to get rid of possessions. Owning stuff just slows you down, weighs you down."

Our baggage can get pretty heavy when we wrap it up in obligations, goals, anxieties, politics, or insecurities. When that happens, take a step back and think of what Segarra and Richards said. We don't have to allow ourselves to be so controlled by things that don't matter. Remember, you are living. It's more important that you breathe in the fresh air and enjoy it than it is that you risk your life rushing off to yet another meeting that really doesn't matter. Fill your life with meaning, and then you are rich.

"Your most important assets are not material things, things you put in your safe deposit box or the money you put in your bank account," said legendary oceanographer Sylvia Earle. "It's what you have in your mind, your brain. It's what you know, who you are, and the circle of friends and allies you build. Houses can burn, markets can crash, accidents can happen. The things you think are most important can, in a flash, be gone. But, as long as you have your mind and people who care about you and people who you care about, you can do anything. It takes imagination, skill, and initiative."

Earle is often called "Her Royal Deepness" or the "Carl Sagan of our Oceans." She has led more than 50 expeditions and spent more than 6,000 hours diving, but her passion for preserving the environment has stood out above all of her achievements. She advocates loudly and fervently for the oceans and the environment, and in 1998, *Time* magazine named her its first "Hero for the Planet."

What are you doing to make this world better? "If you don't do or say anything, then you are part of the problem," Earle said. "If you, in your heart, disagree and just go along without saying anything, you are speaking through your silence. Your voice is silent, and others are speaking for you. I am so frustrated with people who say, 'What can I, as one person do? Any change that has ever happened has always started with one person doing something. Then it is two people, then 10 people, then 15, then 1,000 moving in one direction."

You are never alone, even if the people in your circle don't agree with you, she said. "Take a small step. A little step makes a difference. It always, always makes a difference. You may not appreciate how important it is. Too many decisions are made by default by those who choose not to take that small step to protect the things they love. They leave it to somebody else, assuming somebody else is looking out for clean water, for the education of their children, or whatever the issue is that they care about. But you can't count on anybody else being out there to take up your slack."

Take up your own slack. Be a mustang.

In conclusion . . .

WOMAN,
BE
BOLD.

Index

About the Author

Fawn Germer's first book, *Hard Won Wisdom,* stormed out of the gate and onto the bestseller list despite a release date shortly after the 9-11 tragedies. The book was buoyed by this four-time Pulitzer nominee's ability to connect so well with live audiences. After *Oprah* featured her book and Oprah Winfrey told her audience of its "very inspiring" message, Germer gained notice as one of the nation's most sought-after speakers.

This acclaimed investigative reporter has worked as a Florida correspondent for both the *Washington Post* and *U.S. News and World Report.* Her distinguished reporting career earned her numerous state and national awards including the prestigious Green Eyeshade Award from the Society for Professional Journalists. She has been a staff writer for the *Miami Herald,* Denver's *Rocky Mountain News,* and the *Florida Times-Union* in Jacksonville. She was an editor for the *Tampa Tribune* and has written for *Working Woman, Redbook, Cosmopolitan,* and the *American Journalism Review.*

In addition, Germer is founder of the Author's Retreat, where new writers consult with Germer in order to put their book projects on the fast track through the obstacle course of the publishing world.

Contact the Author

Bestselling author Fawn Germer works with organizations that want more courageous and creative performance from their people. Using the success secrets and strategies from the hundreds of leaders she's interviewed, Germer teaches brass-tacks boldness.

Germer has keynoted events for Motorola, Capital One, Boeing, the National Reconnaissance Office, JP Morgan Chase, Lifetime TV, and hundreds of other companies and organizations.

For more information on the women in this book or to book Germer for your event:

Telephone: (727) 824-7705
E-mail: info@hardwonwisdom.com
Website: www.hardwonwisdom.com